**JOAN'S CAREER WAS AT ITS LOWEST EBB
WHEN SHE DECIDED TO STAR IN THE FILM
OF HER SISTER'S BESTSELLER, *THE STUD* . . .**

Joan took a great deal of critical heat for having
made such a lurid picture, especially for the orgy
scene in which she hopped on the swing and went
sailing over a pool full of writhing bodies. That is the
only scene she refuses to defend. She felt uncomfortable with it from the start, and wanted to wear a
towel, but, she says, her husband told her "it was a
copout. He tells me I have a great body, so what the
hell?" But it got worse once they started shooting.
Says Joan, "Usually when you do a nude scene, it's
just you and another actor on a closed set. But the
orgy was shot at a completely open pool, so there was
no way to block the technicians." In order to do the
scene, Joan says she got drunk—which only made
things worse, since she "did things I normally
wouldn't do."

**JOAN COLLINS
THE UNAUTHORIZED BIOGRAPHY**

JOAN COLLINS:
THE UNAUTHORIZED BIOGRAPHY

Jeff Rovin

BANTAM BOOKS
TORONTO • NEW YORK • LONDON • SYDNEY • AUCKLAND

JOAN COLLINS: THE UNAUTHORIZED BIOGRAPHY
A Bantam Book / March 1985

ISBN 0-553-17163-1

Published simultaneously in the United States and Canada

Bantam Books are published by Bantam Books, Inc. Its trademark,
consisting of the words "Bantam Books" and the portrayal of a
rooster, is registered in U.S. Patent and Trademark Office and in
other countries. Marca Registrada. Bantam Books, Inc., 666 Fifth
Avenue, New York, New York 10103.

Printed and bound in Great Britain by Hunt Barnard Printing Ltd.

O   0 9 8 7 6 5 4 3 2 1

"There are a lot of famous 'JCs,'
starting with Jesus Christ."

—Joan Collins

Introduction

◆◆◆◆◆◆◆◆◆◆◆◆◆◆◆◆◆◆◆◆◆◆◆◆◆◆◆◆◆◆◆◆◆◆◆◆◆

Johnny Carson clasped his hands behind his back, puffed out his chest, and sniggered in his boyish way, "We have Joan Collins with us tonight . . . and she's going to make a startling revelation. Joan is going to tell us that she plans to marry again—as soon as the Oakland Raiders get their freedom."

The audience laughed at Carson's quip, one of those fill-in-the-blank gags into which the name of the latest much-divorced actress is plugged. Weak as the joke was, however, longtime admirers of Joan Collins took perverse satisfaction in seeing their heroine enshrined in a way previously reserved for the likes of Liz, Zsa Zsa, and other entertainment legends. It had taken the actress a long time, but against all odds she'd finally reached Mecca, achieving a state of instant recognition.

When the jokes were finished and Collins came on, she demonstrated just how comfortably she wore the crown of a queen. She swaggered out as though she owned not only the stage but the audience and cameras as well. And for the duration of her visit, Joan rarely looked at Johnny or at anything else in particular: she presented profiles, struck poses, and let the lens drink her up. If she wanted to express an emotion she did it through body language, especially her shoulders. She shrugged them girlishly to soften an off-color quip, arched them catlike to indicate dissatisfaction, rolled them to and fro like a quarterback settling in for the snap whenever she meant business, and raised one sharply to underline her indignation over an unpleasant event she was describing. Her shoulders moved so that her face didn't have to, frozen behind a thick mask of makeup—a heavy layer of foundation to smooth out her fifty-one-year-old skin, deep shadow to highlight her eyes and false lashes to make them sultry, lips glossed a sleek chrome red. The only expression that came through was a hint of bemusement, as though the actress were perpetually on the verge of blowing the viewer one of those big, wet, movie-star kisses which says, *I love you, but not nearly as much as you love me.* Through it all came the persona Joan Collins wished to present, the living version of the Joan Collins portrayed in her fun, peppery autobiography, *Past Imperfect*, published by Simon and Schuster.

The conversation with Johnny was artificial. As soon as she was seated, Joan gushed to Johnny, "I haven't seen you since—*Oscar* night," using the slight pause before "Oscar" to suggest that she went to so many grand events she had difficulty keeping them straight. Of course, before she became Alexis Carrington on *Dynasty*, Joan Collins was rarely considered important enough to invite to the Academy Awards or, for that matter, to anything bigger than the annual bash thrown by the Count Dracula Society which, in 1975, voted her an acting award for one of her horror films. It was an award that, at the time, she'd been only too happy to accept in person.

Now Collins flits from the Oscars to audiences with Queen Elizabeth, to parties with the likes of Michael Jackson and Shirley MacLaine. And on *The Tonight Show*, as elsewhere, she never forgets that Alexis made it all possible, carefully dropping lines like, "I've always known how to spell Cartier," and, "I never watch football. I'm more into *other* kinds of sports." It isn't just Joan Collins talking but her wealthy, sexual *Dynasty* alter ego—Collins's meal ticket, the person viewers *expect* to see.

Beneath the glamour and affectation, Collins is more interesting by far than Alexis. She's a survivor, a despot, a victim, a bitch, a devoted mother, and often a less than devoted wife. She may work hard to be oh-so-witty in public and, in print, spin a version of her life that is at once one-sided and superficial. But whatever public face she puts on, Joan Collins is above all a phoenix, whose rise from the ashes is not only a compelling saga but one of the most remarkable celebrity tales of our age.

JOAN COLLINS

Chapter One

•••

*S*ince late in the last century, the London districts of Bayswater—situated just north of woodsy Kensington Gardens—and Maida Vale—to its north—have had a character uniquely their own. Nowhere else in the city is there the same dramatic juxtaposition of quiet, tree-lined residential streets and those cluttered with commerce. There is constant motion throughout: pedestrians shopping or strolling, vehicles moving swiftly past the regal apartments and hotels which line broad avenues like Bayswater Road and Maida Vale. They edge slowly past the markets, underground stations, and stores, which stand shoulder to shoulder along the narrower side streets.

Both parts of town are considered "comfortable" by the locals, neither rundown nor exclusive. Above all they offer their residents a pleasant environment as well as convenience, factors that surely appealed to Joseph William Collins when he and his wife, the former Elsa Bessant, moved into a flat in Maida Vale. A theatrical agent, Collins was attracted by the easy access to the theaters and clubs, whose new acts he might want to see for possible representation. For her part, Elsa was delighted to be just a short walk from both Regent's Park, a half-mile to the east, and Hyde

1

Park, nearly a mile to the south. A former dancer, she enjoyed stretching her legs on pleasant mornings.

Though the country was in the middle of the Depression, Joe was doing well enough. Having come to England and established Collins and Grade with Lew Grade (now Lord Lew Grade, one of the great entrepreneurs of the English stage and screen) he was kept busy providing comedians, magicians, dancers, singers, and jugglers to a public anxious to forget how miserable they were.

Elsa, retired from the stage and domesticized by her good-natured but traditional husband, had little in common with the friends she had made in the theater, or with most of Joe's old chums and business acquaintances. Thus, when daughter Joan Henriette Collins was born on May 23, 1933, she became Elsa's entire life.

Joan was born in a nursing home at 268 Gloucester Terrace in Bayswater's Paddington subdistrict. In a more fanciful tale, it might be said that she drank up the contrasts of her environment. Certainly her mother found her to be a bundle of energy and impishness and, even though she had a nanny almost from the start, Joan was still a handful for the doting Elsa. As Joan's mother later put it, "Somewhere along the way Joan developed an absolute genius for the unexpected."

Some of this precocity was instilled in Joan by her paternal grandmother. Henrietta Asenheim had been a vaudeville actress/dancer in Cape Town, South Africa, when she met Isaac Hart, the booking manager of a big music hall circuit. Hart, who changed his name to the less Jewish-sounding Collins, took Henrietta as his bride and, in 1902, Joseph was born.

"Hetty," as Henrietta was known, was a spirited lady right up until her death in her late eighties, and she gave a lot of that spunk to her granddaughter. She was especially proud of having taught Joan how to do crude cartwheels and splits not long after the girl learned to walk—much to the chagrin of Elsa, who was working hard to raise a "sweet and lovely young lady" and not, as she later came to call her, "Miss Perpetual Motion."

When the outgoing little girl asked to attend dancing school before she was quite three, Elsa was hardly surprised, though she was torn. It would be excellent discipline for Joan, yet neither she nor Joe wanted to see a third generation of Collinses in show business. Joe had been in the industry since 1917, when he'd started tacking handbills to trees for his father, and both parents knew how difficult it was to achieve even modest success in the field. As Elsa later said, they wanted to protect her from the "hardships and heartbreaks involved." But that was only part of their reserve. Despite the fact that Hetty, Elsa, and Joe's two sisters had all been on the stage, it was not considered a terribly respectable profession for a woman. The Collinses, relocated in London, where opportunity was greater than it had been in South Africa, saw no reason for Joan to pursue such a career.

At the time, however, Joan's fascination was considered more or less innocent. In fact, her father derived great pleasure from her gregarious nature, in large part because it was closer to his own personality than to that of the demure, domestic Elsa. Whether it was making her stage debut in a nursery school play at the age of three or hamming it up in public, he enjoyed it all, never imagining then how damaging it would be to Joan if at some point he wasn't around to laugh at her antics and encourage her self-expression.

Her mother was understandably less enthusiastic since she was the one who had to keep Joan under control. "Even when Joan was predictable the atmosphere was a lively one," she stated. "We were in a department store once when Joan was three, when a floor full of fellow shoppers began to scream with laughter. I glanced around to find the source of amusement. Her name was Miss Collins and she was as busy as could be taking hats off the stands, trying them on, and mimicking the models perfectly."

As the years passed, Joe's encouragement of his daughter's talents moderated, since it occurred to her parents that their daughter's interest might not be a passing fancy: virtually everything she did was in some way related to entertainment. When Joan learned how to operate the record player, she danced for hours; even the dolls she collected were not just the normal cuddly type but frenetic figures sculpted in a variety of dancing poses. She was also fond of drawing, and when sister Jackie, six years her junior, started writing short stories, Joan was only too happy to sit down with pencils and crayons and provide the illustrations. Years later, the sisters would literally save each other's career by teaming again, this time on a pair of do-or-die motion pictures.

Given her interests, it's not surprising that Joan's earliest ambition was to become "a great ballerina or an artist living in a garret." But that changed when she discovered radio dramas. Though she had always listened to musical programs and danced to whatever was playing, she grew increasingly more fascinated by the radio plays. "I used to sit mesmerized and my imagination took over totally," she says. Her favorite program was *Dick Barton*, about a private investigator, and his aides Jock and Snowy. In fact, when Joan received a detective set one Christmas she pretended to be a sleuth for months thereafter, "going round the house and picking up fingerprints, testing to see if anyone had been through my personal possessions." Even when she outgrew the kit, Joan would improvise playlets about detectives, families, celebrities, and anyone else that came to mind, performing with herself, her sister, or whomever would take a role.

However, the most important influence on Joan's early years was motion pictures. From the day she saw her first film, movies became her passion—much more so than music or dance or radio melodramas. She made someone take her to the cinema a minimum of three times a week, and she diligently kept a scrapbook of stars' pictures and autographs. Her collection eventually grew to fill several thick volumes, mostly signed pictures she'd obtained by writing to the studios, as well as others collected by her father whenever his work brought him into contact with a star. As testimony to Joan's remarkable will, those stars who did *not* respond to her request for an autograph were inscribed in a mental list which she remembered for years. When she was twenty-nine, she actually confided to a reporter that she *still* had bad feelings about John Payne for having ignored the four letters she had sent him.

As Joan later realized, part of her fascination with actors and acting was that someone could be what they weren't. Throughout her childhood, for instance, she'd had a strong desire to be a boy. Her father had wanted a son—hence "Joan" in lieu of "Joe, Jr."—and although Joan never felt unwanted, she found that she "hated the whole idea of becoming a woman. I was quite keen to become masculine, and when I was acting I could play a part." This need would be further accentuated when brother Bill arrived in 1947 and Joan had to compete with a real son for her father's attention. At the time, however, her preoccupation with acting was still relatively harmless, and far less troublesome to the Collins family than a concurrent event—the coming of the Second World War.

Joan was seven years old when the bombing of London commenced on September 7, 1940. On that afternoon, one thousand German planes set out across the Channel, meeting virtually no resistance from the unprepared British and leaving 1,600 Londoners dead or injured, and much of the city covered with smoke and rubble. As if that were not enough, 250 bombers returned that night, moving methodically over the English capital and setting street after street ablaze.

The Luftwaffe made nightly attacks on London for nearly two months thereafter, and then sporadically for the rest of the year. Each time the air raid sirens sounded, Londoners left their homes and headed for the underground railway stations, which served as crowded, airless shelters.

During this time life at the Collins home, as elsewhere, was a shambles. Joan remembers vividly, "I scarcely ever slept a whole night in one bed. Mother put me to bed in a zippered suit, 'siren suits' they were called, and the next thing I knew I was being awakened and carried to an air raid shelter. I still have nightmarish memories of sleeping in the London tubes while German Stukas dropped bombs near us." Once, she says, she was carried from her bed moments before a bomb made a direct hit next door. "After the 'all clear,'" she continues, "my nursery looked like a giant matchbox—nothing but splinters. Even now," she adds, "I leave the living room lights on when I go to sleep."

Apart for the material losses the Collinses suffered, Elsa and her daughters were constantly being separated from Joe. "London became too hot a target," Joan says, "so Mother took Jackie and me all over England to escape the bombing." Unfortunately, Joe had to stay behind since business, ironically, was booming. It was not simply a matter of owing it to his clients to arrange for them to work: it was a matter of patriotism as well. The English needed to laugh and be entertained while their world was falling apart, and he was the man who could make it happen.

For the next few years, Joan and her sister were

shuttled between the city and villages that lay from one to four hours outside London. Being constantly on the move made the fidgety Joan even more restless—"like a desert Arab," she later described herself—and she grew from a plucky child into a stubborn, headstrong adolescent. Then, too, while those places were far from the fiery horror of the blitz, they weren't as idyllic as names like Ilfracombe and Bognor suggest. Says Joan, "I still remember my chagrin when all during the summer I was at a school near the beach and was forbidden to go in swimming because of mines."

The principal targets of Joan's blossoming independence were her teachers. Because of the war, Joan was forced to attend thirteen different schools. And while most of the transfers were war-related, as she went from London to the countryside and back again, the one notable exception was when she was expelled for smoking at the age of ten. Fittingly, the only lesson Joan seemed to learn was to be more discreet when it came to cigarettes.

Despite the expulsion, Joan was constantly pitting her will against that of her teachers. "I hated school," she admits, maintaining that all one ever got from study was "squinty eyes." She found Latin and math particularly boring, though her lackadaisical attitude wasn't limited to the classroom. She had no use for sports, showing only a fair affinity for swimming (despite one of her first studio press releases which described her as "an expert swimmer") and was downright "lazy when it came to netball and lacrosse." This did not endear her to her teammates which, in turn, made Joan care even less about them. Perhaps things would have been better had she been in one place long enough to join cliques and make new friends. But that never happened and, in the all-girls schools she attended, either one was an insider or an outsider—and Joan was always the latter.

A great deal of Joan's rebelliousness also derived from the fact that she was constantly away from her father, the "soul mate" to whom she often wished she could turn. Joan had no one to fawn over her, to protect her. Elsa, though extremely loving and gentle, wasn't as demonstrative as Joe, and certainly didn't understand her as well. Then there was also the displeasure she felt with the way she looked. In her early teens Joan had no color and was extremely thin; she thought her eyes were too large, and she did not like the unflattering Dutch bob she wore. As if dissatisfaction with her looks wasn't bad enough, she resented the bland school uniform she was forced to wear, a gray outfit with a maroon tie and long black stockings.

Through it all, the arts in general and movies in particular remained Joan's sanctuary. She kept up her scrapbooks, and when she couldn't see movies or read about their stars she lost herself in novels, hiding "penny dreadfuls" behind her schoolbooks. She also continued her dancing lessons, attending ten different academies during the war years, though by this time dance was more like work than play and she was less enthusiastic about it than she had been as a child. Above all, her objective was somehow to survive the oppressive boredom of school, and she dreamt of the day when she would reach the age of sixteen and could put it all behind her.

Just what she would do then wasn't really in doubt—at least, not to Joan. The one bright spot in her entire educational career was the semester at the Cone-Ripman School when she took her first drama course. It was the closest she had ever come to real acting, and it was like a life raft to her. But the seas were storm-tossed from the start. Among the first things the instructor told her students was, "Not one of you will ever make an actress," a comment designed to separate ambitious youths from those who were there for a lark. Joan took the remark as a personal attack and, unable to sleep at all that night, told herself over and over that she would prove the drama mistress dead wrong, that she *would* make it as an actress. And so she did. Alone among the entire class, Joan was chosen to dress up in a sailor suit and appear on the stage of London's Arts Theater in a small part in Henrik Ibsen's *A Doll's House*—ironically, as Nora's *son*. Unfortunately, whether she was bored by the simplicity of the part, or was subconsciously looking to call attention to her entrance, on the night of the play Joan stood in the wings reading a trashy novel and missed her cue. She says, "John Fernald, the producer, almost had a fit. He turned a fine purple and swore he'd never again have children in a play."

Nonetheless, when she'd gotten her act together and stepped onstage, Joan was hooked. She couldn't see the audience because of the lights, but she knew they were out there looking at her, being entertained by her. It was attention and glamour bundled in a neat package and, hungry for both, she knew that this was where she belonged.

Chapter Two

When the family was reunited after the war, they moved into a sprawling building known as Harley House, located just to the east of their old flat, and still one of the area's most imposing structures. Six stories tall and built of large

fawn-colored blocks, the ornate old structure is situated near the end of Marylebone Road, a two-minute
walk from Regent's Park and just a few doors beyond
Madame Tussaud's wax museum. There are several
entrances leading into the block-long building from
Marylebone, each fronted with pillars and colorful
cement planters. However, the Collinses didn't have
a flat accessible by the front door. As though reflect-
ing the low regard many people had for the theater,
they lived in rooms in the basement, the entrance to
which was a dark stairwell that vanished into the
concrete behind a low iron fence. With windows that
barely rose above the street, the flat was dark and
usually chilly—a fitting environment for what turned
out to be a dreary homecoming.

The real problem, of course, was not the subterra-
nean flat but the way in which Joan's relationship
with her father had changed. Her mother was still
there, as she'd always been and would be until her
untimely death, but that wasn't enough. Elsa had
always been there, doting and giving. It was her
father's attention Joan wanted but, unfortunately, his
approval, like his criticism, was given in extremes.

When Joan was an only child, and an adorable one
to boot, she had had a monopoly on Joe. Later, she
learned to share the spotlight with baby Jackie and
the war, which was a bother but not a traumatic one.
Then Bill was born, and the son Joe had always
wanted utterly displaced both girls. Joan put up a
fight for a while, focusing her energies on endearing
herself to Joe. She tried to enjoy the baby *with* him,
and when that didn't broaden the spotlight to include
her, she withdrew from Bill and pursued a different
tack. She tried to get closer to her father by pre-
tending to be interested in the things he enjoyed,
such as sports and even poker, but the effort was too
great and the results negligible. She couldn't compete
with a baby and, acting be damned, she couldn't be a

boy. This was truer than it had been years before when she'd played detective for now, if nothing else, at the age of fifteen Joan was physically a woman.

To make matters worse, as a result of her scholastic independence, Joan finished her years of academic bondage with a stunning setback. Sitting for her school certificate in 1949 she failed badly, ending all those years of schooling without a diploma. That made her feel, in her words, "very insecure about my intellectual capacities. I thought I was very dumb and, in fact, I was." And while she wouldn't— indeed, *couldn't*—have done things differently, the combination of isolation at home and rejection in the classroom left her feeling "a mess."

When all was said and done, her one source of satisfaction had always been show business. She'd succeeded onstage, albeit in a small way, and not only had it felt good to be there but she was actually good at it. Joan believed that with the proper training she'd get even better and, driven by a blend of love and desperation, she elected to try to make it her career.

In the heart of London, at the foot of sedate and sunny Gower Street, is RADA—the Royal Academy of Dramatic Art. From the outside RADA looks more like a shrine than a school with its white granite façade looming behind a black iron fence, and a pair of large graven images flanking the four-panel door. Nor do the stolid high priests, the keepers of the craft, go out of their way to dispel the shrinelike impression. Within its Spartan halls and drab chambers, whose windows are small and prisonlike, RADA trains artists to fill the voracious and exacting appetite of the English stage. Only the best get in, and only the purists *stay* in. RADA frowns on craftspeople who would even consider acting in films, though that hasn't stopped many alumni from making the transition, among them Albert Finney, Peter O'Toole, and Susannah York.

When Joan set her sights on RADA, she was not merely aiming high, she was going up against awesome odds. Of the five hundred or so who apply to RADA each year, only a handful are accepted. Having failed to get her school certificate would also work against her, since RADA frowned on illiterates. She had recently faced so much rejection that a turndown would be like salt in an open wound, a prospect she did not relish. Also, failure would leave her just another aspiring actress all dressed up with nowhere to go. Yet foremost in Joan's mind was that if she *did* make the grade, it would be the euphoric boost she desperately needed. Being nothing if not gutsy, Joan wanted to give herself that chance to succeed. There was just one problem: she had to convince her parents to let her become an actress. If ever she'd felt alone, this was the time.

"Joan did *not* inherit my love for housework and cooking," Elsa Collins once sighed, more amused than upset. "When we were without help during the war, I'd ask her to do this or that in the kitchen, and in her dramatic way she'd counter, 'You know, Mummy, you chose to be a housewife. I didn't.'" Although Joan would invariably pitch in, both parents knew that the domestic life was not for her.

Still, Joe was convinced that as Joan matured she'd grow into it. In the meantime, he reveals, "My idea was for her to be a secretary, or something like that." Despite her awful grades there were schools she could attend to brush up on the requisite skills, and he had no doubt she'd succeed once she set her mind to it. Besides, part of his plan was for her to work in his office, where he could help her settle down and make sure that she began accepting adult responsibilities.

Joe was the one who actually broached the subject of his daughter's future. Troubled by her failure to

obtain a certificate, he and Elsa sat down with her for
a nice heart-to-heart chat, at which time he outlined
his thoughts on a secretarial career. Joan listened, and
when he finished, she made her counterproposal
about RADA.

At first, she remembers, "Father looked at me as if
I'd suggested taking a rocket to the moon," and she
braced herself for a flat-out rejection, not quite
knowing what she'd do when it came. But Joe's
shocked expression faded after a moment and, much
to Joan's utter shock, he smiled and agreed it might
be a good idea for her to try out for RADA. Beside
herself with joy, Joan bounded off, though Elsa
stayed behind, slightly more suspicious.

"I was pretty well floored," she remembered, "and
when we were alone, I politely asked him if he'd lost
his mind."

"Of course not," was Joe's reply. "I think it's a fine
idea."

"But after all the years you've been objecting," she
returned, "I don't understand!"

"Don't you see," he told her, "this will be the
finish. Let her take the exam. She'll never pass it and
that will be the end of it."

Although Elsa appreciated his logic, she appreciated the downside as well: how crushed Joan would
be if she failed. "To bolster Joan's morale," she said,
"and to help soften the blow that I was certain would
come, I took her shopping for a special dress. It was
white with blue polka dots, and Joan went to the
audition feeling as if she had stepped out of *Vogue*."

Getting into RADA was a combination of educational background, a personal interview, and an
audition, the audition being the most critical factor.
Since she felt her bad grades and a good interview
would balance out, Joan concentrated on the audition, ultimately selecting a speech from Bernard
Shaw's *Caesar and Cleopatra* and an entire scene from
Thornton Wilder's *Our Town*.

She remembers being extremely worried the day of the audition, but she managed to get through it, and to get through it well, she thought. That's when the real agony began. It would be weeks before the board—which consisted of staff members as well as such distinguished actors as Laurence Olivier and alumnus John Gielgud—made its decision. In the meantime, says Joan, "I was on tenterhooks." Fortunately, the family had scheduled a vacation immediately after the audition, and Joan was able to push it to the back of her mind as she lolled in the sun at a French seaside resort.

While she was there, she made a discovery that was to provide her with more joy, sorrow, anger, giddiness, and pain than anything else in her life: she discovered men.

"He was Bernard," she says, "a curly-haired French boy whose father owned a string of ice cream shops." Joan met him when she went to buy an ice cream cone one day, and she "fell deeply in love for the first time."

Until Joan encountered Bernard under a broiling summer sun, boys had been a mystery to her. She hadn't met any young men at the all-girls schools she'd attended, and knew only the sketchiest details about sex. However, she had been raised to believe that sketchy details were quite enough. "When I was growing up," she says, "young girls were supposed to behave extremely well and not do naughty things in any way at all. My grandmother was a Victorian, so my mother's attitude toward life was based on Victorianism—which was the most prudish time in life. That's how I grew up, feeling that a young girl shouldn't let a man do anything." That not only included sex but references to sex as well. Joan relates: "My mother told me once that if my father ever said the 'f' word she would divorce him. She was absolutely serious, because I asked her once before that what it meant and she bashed my head against the wall—and she was by nature nonviolent!"

Bernard was her first look at the species and, though her curiosity as whetted, she didn't learn a great deal from him. He spoke no English, she spoke no French and, in any case, they never did anything more daring than stroll along the beach holding hands. Yet his presence was enough to cause Joan, in spite of her prudishness, to "wonder just where boys had been all my life," and she hoped she would learn more when she returned to England. She did, however, learn one thing from Bernard. She says that he gave her "an unlimited amount of ice cream," which started her appetite for gifts. Joan liked getting things from men, something she would miss dearly when she had to pay off this husband or that to get him out of her life.

For years, Joan stuck by the following yarn about her acceptance to RADA, one she had recounted to a publicist on an early film. "They made an exception to the rules by admitting me when I was only fourteen," she said, "instead of the normal entrance age of sixteen or seventeen. This was possible because I came from a theatrical background."

In truth, while the RADA board was aware of her father's work, it was solely the strength of Joan's performance which had gotten her into the academy. And when the letter of acceptance arrived, there was only one person more excited than Joan. According to Elsa, "There was no prouder man in the whole of the British Isles than her father." Not that his attitude toward an acting career had changed; it hadn't, at least not then. Making it into RADA was an impressive achievement, but it wasn't quite the same as making it through RADA and earning a living on the stage. Indeed, while it's fair to say that Joe was happy because Joan had realized her dream, he still found it extremely difficult to see things through her eyes, to accept her ideas as having any validity.

Regardless, as the summer of 1949 drew to a close, Joe was happy, his daughter was ecstatic and, for a while—a very *short* while—all was right with the world.

Chapter Three

◆◆◆◆◆◆◆◆◆◆◆◆◆◆◆◆◆◆◆◆◆◆◆◆◆◆◆◆◆◆◆◆◆◆◆◆◆◆

*T*hroughout most of her early life, Joan Collins didn't want for necessities. Even with all the moving about and rationing during the war, the Collinses lived comfortably. Still, she never lived the kind of life she envied, the glamourous life of a film star; she didn't even come close. Her father was frugal, and only when her mother cajoled did he hand over money for luxuries like jewelry or a new dress for an audition. Their flats were always pleasant, but never more than that; in Harley House, for example, Joan would watch people moving to and from their airy, well-lighted rooms while she lived in the basement. With the proper blend of talent and ambition, acting was a way to have the kind of money she read about in the Hollywood fan magazines.

Beyond the material goods a successful acting career could provide, Joan's desire to be onstage increased as she grew older—not coincidentally in proportion to the dilution of her father's attention. She wasn't driven, like many performers, by boundless narcissism, nor did she have the intellectual curiosity of actors who enjoy scraping around inside the skulls of characters in an effort to understand and interpret them. Joan Collins went into acting to acquire things, goods as well as attention.

Not that she wasn't challenged by acting. When she was sixteen and seventeen, Joan would wait until her parents went out on weekends and, sneaking into her mother's room, apply lipstick and rouge and slip into one of Elsa's more sophisticated outfits. Taking the underground to the center of town, she'd casually walk up to the box office of a theater showing a film for adults only, and try to buy a ticket. The ruse failed as often as it worked, but that wasn't the point. While she enjoyed the forbidden fruit of seeing an "A" film, the ritual of dolling herself up and trying to get in was a night's entertainment in itself.

The objectives of RADA, however, did not include money and attention-getting and no matter how good her readings or how expressive her raw talent, Joan and the academy were a pair of automobiles, sports car and Rolls-Royce, predestined to collide.

Two other forces fated to meet at RADA were Joan and men. Writing about Joan in 1955, *Motion Picture* magazine described her, at seventeen, as "a tearing, fully-packed beauty" and, in a coed situation, it did not take her long to get over the last of what she calls her "tender stage of being an ugly duckling." Boys noticed her and she noticed them. And while she enjoyed the attention of boys who pursued *her*—the conversation, kissing, and hand holding—what really thrilled her was snaring aloof young men or luring out the good-looking introverts. It wasn't just her desire to be with them, but that she perceived these men as more adult, more "fatherly." It was a challenge (like sneaking into an "A" film) and one ripe with delicious opportunities to act more vampishly than she had when trying to be noticed by her father.

Thus, almost from day one at RADA Joan was like a child in a candy shop, flitting to a new goody each week or so. Though her clinging prudishness made for relationships that were all heat and no flame, men were a new world whose horizons she was both anxious and excited to be exploring.

It's interesting to speculate what Joan Collins might have accomplished had she applied herself to RADA with the same dedication she showed for manhunting. But fate plotted against her. A few months after classes had begun, photographers from a line of magazines came to RADA looking for models. They asked to see the ten most beautiful girls in the school, and though RADA officials weren't keen on such publications, it was in their best interest to help their students stay solvent. Thus, they more or less averted their gaze and pitched in when such things came up.

After considering the student body, the photographers selected Joan—not to do fashion set-ups but, as Joan puts it, "to illustrate subjects like girls on the run, teenage mothers, and all sorts of other realistic things like that." The pictures appeared in magazines such as *True Romances* and *True Confessions*.

Though the work wasn't especially glamourous, Joan was thrilled to do it. "It was like the still photographs from a film," she says, "without being in the movie. It called for a bit of acting, and the results were very convincing."

However, whether it was sour grapes, high-hattedness, or both, the other students didn't share Joan's enthusiasm. They gave popular art and its advocates the cold shoulder, and it didn't take long for peer pressure to bring Joan around. She continued to do photo sessions on the side, for pocket money—or so she told her classmates—and entered what she calls her "repulsive period," hanging out with a group that went by the quaint name of the Slobs. As a Slob, Joan says she "went about with lank, uncombed hair, dressing untidily in rumpled clothes, taking too few baths [and] staying up all night swilling black coffee and discussing the 'theat-ah,' art, and life." Joan also grew to "frown on the movies" for being so "crassly commercial," a front that stood far longer than her family expected. If nothing else, it was a tribute to how desperately Joan needed to belong to a crowd.

Despite her esthetic rebirth, Joan's first year at RADA was extremely trying. Never one to worry about posture diction, she was shocked to find that the faculty deemed these qualities as important as acting ability. Since discipline in these areas had never been among Joan's strengths, RADA worked on her poise and voice. Worked her *over* is a more apt description, since Joan never quite grasped why it was necessary to master the basics. She'd always intended to be a free spirit on stage, something of a method actor, performing from instinct and freedom rather than discipline.

But that wasn't the RADA way, and though their gentlemanly manhandling left her feeling "I couldn't act . . . and I didn't know what I was doing," she survived. Much of the credit for that was due to her extracurricular activities, not only the magazine work but her friends.

"I went with the girls when I didn't have a boyfriend," she says, adding impishly, "though mostly I *did* have a boyfriend, even though he changed from week to week." Whoever she was with, Slobs or guys (one of her dates being future *Dallas* rival Larry Hagman, an aspiring actor whom she remembered as "very shy"), their favorite pastime was "spending nights listening to bebop in the jive clubs on Oxford Street. I loved the music," she says fondly, "and I adored dancing there until dawn, even though the newspapers found this pastime something dreadful. They ran stories of the clubs and called them 'dens of iniquity,' hinting at marijuana and dope. But the clubs were nothing like that—at least not the ones I went to." Nor, she says, was that what they wanted. "We London teenagers weren't really bad," says Joan. "On the surface, we pretended to be bohemian and therefore privileged to lead an undisciplined life, but the bohemian look was just a mask." They wore it, she explains, to conceal from themselves, as much as from others, the insecurity any aspiring actor feels about the future and to rebel against the kind of austerity to which they were subjected at RADA. But RADA was their world, and they put on brave faces during the day, let loose a little at night and on weekends, and made the best of things.

By the summer of 1950, Joan was exhausted. However, being on the RADA anvil for a year had left her anxious to put some of what she'd learned to the test. With her father's help, she wangled a job as assistant stage manager with the Maidstone Company in Kent, where she did everything from painting scenery to performing in their stage productions. Unhappily, Joan's repertory debut was less than scintillating. So afraid of making mistakes, Joan created a self-fulfilling prophecy: from the start, whether it was mislaying props or flubbing dialogue, she says, "I made so many boo-boos that I found myself highly unpopular with the group." Their attitude only increased her anxiety, causing Joan to foul things up even worse. Between RADA and now Maidstone, the young actress was actually beginning to believe "I was born to be in trouble."

The man who finally managed to restore Joan's fading sense of self-worth was an agent by the name of Bill Watts. Joan later said of him, "He works very hard for his clients and really takes a personal interest in them rather than just in his commission"—qualities she was lucky to find in an often carnivorous breed. From his office in Mayfair, London's poshest area, Watts spent part of each day scouring magazines and films alike for young talent. Spotting a fashion layout Joan had done for *Woman's Own*, he tracked her down and phoned her home. Though Joan still professed that she no longer had any interest in movies, she accepted his invitation to lunch. They met at his office, after which the agent took the seventeen-year-old to one of the fanciest restaurants in town. In spite of herself, she was impressed.

Somewhat more high-powered than her own agent-father, Watts looked Joan up and down and without mincing words said confidently, "I can get you into films, but you'll have to smarten up." When Joan asked what he meant, he replied bluntly, "Your hair's too long and needs a shampoo, your dress could stand a pressing, and you're much too dirty."

Joan smiled condescendingly, amused that Watts hadn't understood that she was an *artiste*. She patiently explained that while she appreciated his interest, her only ambition was to stay at RADA for two years, go from there to a repertory company, and thence into legitimate theater. The truth of the matter was that Joan still wanted to be in movies and she knew it, but she had found a home with the Slobs and didn't want to give that up.

Reading her perfectly, Watts commended Joan's ambition but between soup and dessert convinced her that as crassly commercial as movies were, the exposure would help her career, the money would be good, and above all she would get to practice her craft in a way that would complement rather than neutralize her RADA training.

As much as she wanted to say no, Joan found it impossible. Confused and haunted by images of Pola Negri, Gloria Swanson, Marlene Dietrich, Corinne Griffith, and other film actresses she much admired,

Joan agreed to let him represent her. She promised to come to any auditions properly dressed and scrubbed, but informed him that she would continue being a Slob and taking her craft seriously the rest of the time. Watts had no objection—at least, not then.

Once she had signed with Watts, events moved quickly. Within a matter of days she was at Shepperton Studios in southwest London, being screen-tested for the leading role in *Lady Godiva Rides Again*, a contemporary tale about the dark side of beauty contests.

A screen test was, and remains, the most critical factor in determining whether a fresh face gets a part in a film or whether a seasoned film star can play something totally different from anything he's done before. That someone can act is no guarantee he'll look good when projected forty feet tall: the screen test—literally a filmed audition—helps the producers and director make that determination.

Lady Godiva Rides Again was being directed by Frank Launder, who would later make a name for himself with the popular series of films about St. Trinian's, and while he didn't select Joan for the starring role, he thought enough of her screen test to give her a bit part as a beauty contestant. Not bad for just a week out of the gate! Nor did Watts let up. A few weeks later he got her a slightly meatier part in *The Woman's Angle*, followed by an even larger role in a crime drama called *Judgment Deferred*.

Joan's parts in all of these pictures were shot on holidays during her second year at RADA. Each stint lasted just a few days, never interfering with her classes. So while RADA didn't approve, it was forbearing—even when reviews of Joan's films and captions under newspaper photographs singled out her sex appeal instead of her acting ability. Joan herself winced when she read press releases from *Judgment Deferred* which boasted—prematurely, she thought candidly—"BRILLIANT NEW SCREEN DISCOVERY! When two such experienced veterans of the film industry as John Baxter [producer-director] and Bill Watts think they have discovered a future star, then it's something to talk about. Joan Collins is the girl!" But RADA's patience was stretched to the limit when Joan was considered for a fourth film, a major production entitled *I Believe in You*.

I Believe in You was the story of how a probation officer handles the parolees in his jurisdiction, and Joan was being considered for the featured part of Norma, a young delinquent. Though Joan's previous screen work had been in a more glamourous vein, her confession magazine spreads led the producers to believe she could handle the role. Still, the film-makers wanted to do a test of Joan dressed in a nightgown and doing something cheap, just to be sure. They set it up with Watts, and though the appointment happened to fall during school hours, the agent was not about to change it. Director Basil Dearden was a heavyweight in the English cinema, having directed such classics as *Halfway House*, *Saraband*, and the brilliant prisoner-of-war drama *The Captive Heart*, starring Michael Redgrave. Producer Michael Relph was equally distinguished, having recently capped a string of hits with the Alec Guinness masterpiece, *Kind Hearts and Coronets*. The men were considered "starmakers," and when they set up a test starlets made it a point to be there.

Joan wasn't happy to hear about the arrangements, since up until then she had managed to have her cake and eat it, too, picking up some $50 per film and still managing to do the work at RADA. Now came a moment of truth: she had to choose between crass commercialism and art. Though she wanted to do the film, she'd become enough of a Slob to think twice about it; attempting to pass the buck, she went to the principal and asked him to excuse her from classes so she could take the test. He dismissed the idea perforce, and it was his arrogant intransigence which finally decided her. "I simply seethed," Joan remembers, "so I cut classes to make the test."

As it turned out, that test was just the first of three Joan would make for *I Believe in You*. These covered not only Norma's tawdry side but her emotionally volatile nature as well. The filmmakers seemed to like her, but Dearden was a thoughtful man when it came to casting his pictures and took his time making a decision. As the third test happened to fall on a holiday, Joan went with her family for a short trip to the South of France. She was aware that if she didn't get the part, she might well have nothing: she says she was "in hot water" with RADA for cutting classes, and wasn't convinced that she had much of a future there.

Fortunately, Joan relates, "When I got back home there was a telegram waiting for me which read, 'Thought you might like to know you've got the part,' signed by Michael Relph." Years later, looking back on her career, Joan confided to an interviewer that reading the telegram was the most exciting moment of her life. It was indeed a triumph for the relatively inexperienced eighteen-year-old, but the euphoria was short-lived. Compared to the ups and downs and disappointments which awaited her in films, even the dismal summer at Maidstone would have to be regarded as a roaring success.

Chapter Four

❖❖❖❖❖❖❖❖❖❖❖❖❖❖❖❖❖❖❖❖❖❖❖❖❖❖❖❖❖❖❖❖❖❖❖❖❖

*T*wo weeks after receiving the telegram—which Joan erroneously remembers as having come from Dearden—she was shooting *I Believe in You*, playing Norma, a teenager on parole.

Ultimately, while the film would not rank among Dearden's most noteworthy pictures, *I Believe in You* did get good notices and make money. However, it did far more for Joan, whom critics singled out for her powerful sexuality: an example of an actress living onscreen what she was afraid to do in her private life.

I Believe in You was produced by Sir Michael Balcon's Ealing Studios, which specialized in films that, in the words of Peter Ustinov, "glorified the small." Although Ealing was autonomous in terms of the movies it made, the company was largely financed by the Rank Organization, one of the most powerful production entities in film history. Until his death in 1972, the Rank Organization was headed by its founder, flour heir J. Arthur Rank, later Lord Arthur Rank, although he was more commonly referred to by friends and foes alike as "King Arthur." After entering the business in 1933, it took him less than a decade to control the production and distribution of the lion's share of films Britons saw, as well as over a thousand of the theaters in which they saw them. The imprimatur of Rank's films, a muscle man striking a sonorous gong, quickly became known worldwide.

Rank and his people were not unaware of Joan's beauty, but her excellent notices convinced them that she was a good bet for films. Thus, they offered her a five-year contract which would start her at nearly $100 a week—increasing to $200 once she proved herself—to make whatever films the studio selected for her. At the same time, like a funhouse version of RADA, they would send Joan to teachers who would show her how to look and act in order to make a better impression on film.

Watts was in favor of the contract, for although it left Joan a slave to Rank, one couldn't have a more influential taskmaster. Joan was concerned that she'd have virtually no say in the pictures she made. But in England, as in Hollywood, that was how the "studio system" worked; and for all its flaws it remained the surest road to stardom. Studios were willing to invest the time necessary to develop a star only if the actor promised to stick around so they could reap the benefits. Despite her misgivings, Joan signed with Rank and gave up her ambition to become a stage actress. She had no choice, really, for RADA would surely have looked without favor on any request to skip classes so that she could make a movie or meet with Rank's glamour coaches.

However, fate conspired against Joan. Shortly after she signed with Rank, the British film industry suffered a sudden and unexpected loss of its audience. Television had grown beyond anyone's expectations, and it took a heavy toll at the box office. Teenagers became the driving economic force in the industry, which compelled English filmmakers to make a great many insipid, youth-oriented films.

Having no voice in the films she made, Joan ended up in many of these exploitation pictures, playing variations of the Norma role: Renee in *Cosh Boy*, as a young thug's girlfriend; Frankie in the boxing drama *The Square Ring*; a prostitute complete with a slit skirt in *Turn the Key Softly*; an unmarried mother in *The*

Good Die Young. Joan quickly tired of these cookie-cutter parts, and no doubt imagined her former RADA colleagues laughing behind her back, snickering as she played tart after tart while they tackled Oliver Goldsmith and Oscar Wilde. But she was too new in the business to do anything about it and, in the beginning, had to content herself with putting her foot down in small ways, such as disapproving of the way the makeup was done and insisting that she be permitted to do her own. ("I was appalled by all the makeup they plastered on," she huffed; "about three inches of horrid slop on my face. A lot of actresses never take it off properly and have terrible skin as a result.")

When months passed and the roles failed to improve, or disappeared altogether, because of the industry-wide recession, Joan grew a little bolder. When she did work she often argued with her directors, trying to instill nuance and depth into her parts. In fact, she was so rude to one director that Watts "blew his stack," according to Joan. But the actress couldn't care less, casually informing her agent, "If people dislike me, that's too bad. The director seemed an awful bore to me."

Though she was beginning to show the kind of spunk no studio will tolerate, the Rank people put up with Joan because she was news. As the only actress they had signed in over a year—and a beautiful one at that—she received an enormous amount of publicity. Because of her delinquent roles she became known in the press as "Britain's Bad Girl," and every time she showed a bit too much cleavage in a photograph the papers steamed with indignation . . . running the offending shot across several columns. Joan hadn't minded this at first, since it brought customers into the theaters. But when the critics stopped taking her seriously and joined the flap, she decided it was time to take a stand.

"Even a moron could see that the 'bad-girl-going-downhill' roles were killing me as an actress," she explains. "At first the critics were kind, calling me England's most promising young actress . . . 'the vest-pocket Ava Gardner' . . . provocative, sex-appealing and so fascinating." She continues bitterly, "Then they began taking potshots at me, saying I was building a career on sexy pin-up poses instead of diversified film roles. Though most of the criticism wasn't personal, it stung just the same." Her tantrums became more frequent, resulting not only in battles with Rank but even "verbal scraps" with Watts. She says, "I was serious about my career, so I spoke my piece over being thrown into the same old mold which turns out so many young actresses as carbon copies of one another. I wanted vivid and tempestuous parts in which I could really act and wear glamorous gowns, because, finally, my repulsive period had ended; I loved wearing smart clothes and spending time on grooming." But she didn't get those roles, and ended up "fighting with the studio over each dreary role for which the wardrobe mistress scoured the secondhand shops for my clothes." She admits having become positively "defiant under criticism, strong-willed, saying whatever I felt like saying whenever I wanted to say it."

In time, even the publicity-hungry Rank Organization tired of her antics and started cracking the whip. Joan remembers bitterly, "They suspended me one time, and another time they substituted another leading lady after filming started. They tried to discipline me by giving me no work for eight months." All that accomplished was to strengthen Joan's resolve, her mother remembering her becoming so frustrated that she "wanted to be released from her contract." (Elsa recalled the moment for more reasons than Joan's state of mind. "We were waiting for a cab," she said, "and Joan's voice was an anguished wail. 'Do you really *want* me to go on being a juvenile delinquent, Mummy? Because I'll do it if you want me to.' I turned around to find every single soul in the vicinity glaring at me as if I were intent on pushing my child into a life of crime.")

The reasonable Elsa understood Joan's problem, but counseled that she wait awhile. Though Joan was genuinely afraid that Rank would ruin her career, she took her mother's advice. There were, as it happened, more pressing concerns on the domestic front.

During this period, most of Joan's unrest was due not only to the films she was doing but to the utter shambles she'd managed to make of her private life.

Surprisingly, it wasn't the pressure at Rank that caused the trouble. Those problems, being what one magazine called "The 3 S girl—a sultry, sexy, siren," reached a boil over a period of two years. On the other hand, her personal affairs took off and exploded like a Roman candle.

Among the stars whom Joan adored in her youth was a striking, six-foot-three-inch actor named Maxwell Reed. Her mother remembered that from the time Joan was fourteen, Reed "was her secret love. She'd casually ask if I would take her to see his films. By the time we'd seen one of them three times, I suspected that there was a crush involved. Then his picture appeared in her locker at school, and another beside her bed."

Reed had the kind of nomadic, adventuresome nature which bred so many of the dashing leading men of this era, from Errol Flynn to Laurence Harvey. Reed was born in Larne, Ireland, on April 2, 1919, the son of a boat builder. At the age of fifteen, becoming bored with school, he decided to go to sea, and spent a great deal of time sailing under Captain "Potato" Jones, helping him run Spanish blockades to get supplies to the hard-pressed Republicans during the Civil War.

Prompted by his parents' pleas, Reed came home after two years to complete his education, and began

performing in school plays to relieve the tedium.
Much to his surprise, he enjoyed the stage so much
that he decided to make acting his career. After
auditioning successfully at RADA, he was there only
four months when the Second World War erupted.
Then, joining the Royal Air Force, he piloted planes
on antisubmarine patrol, though he was discharged
after hitting a buoy while landing in a heavy fog. He
signed up with the Merchant Navy in 1941 and spent
the rest of the war at sea.

Reed then decided not to go back to RADA but
joined the Scarborough Repertory Company. Unlike
his colleagues, who had a low regard for movies,
Reed applied for work as an extra at the Gains-
borough Studios and was delighted to do whatever
films came his way. When he actually talked producer
Sydney Box into giving him a screen test, Reed scored
so highly that he was immediately given a leading
role in a 1946 picture entitled *Daybreak*, the story of a
young couple's infidelity. When they met Reed was
well on his way to becoming a star, unlike Joan, who
had just signed with Rank. With a dozen films to his
credit, he'd gone so far as to form Maxwell Reed
Enterprises in 1948, whose purpose was to manage
his financial affairs.

Joan and Reed met in January 1952. Joan was on a
date with Laurence Harvey, who had acted with her
in *I Believe in You*, and they'd gone to a party at
a fashionable restaurant called La Rue when she
spotted Reed, with whom Harvey had also recently
appeared in *There Is Another Sun*. As soon as Joan saw
him, her heart started slamming hard against her
throat and she asked Harvey to introduce her. When
she gazed into Reed's piercing gray-green eyes,
which were framed by devilishly arched brows, Joan
was immediately hooked. Elsa later commented that
he quite "swept her off her feet."

The two chatted for a while, the eighteen-year-old
actress nearly swooning whenever he flashed his

cheek-splitting smile. She tried hard to appear sophisticated, smoking incessantly as the suave Reed, drawing casually on American cigarettes, regaled her with stories about his adventures and his impressions of Hollywood, where he had just filmed *Flame of Araby* with Maureen O'Hara (not, as Joan has reported, Ann Blyth). Joan passed the evening as though she were waltzing through a dream, and when he called the next day to ask her for a date, she accepted at once. Aware that her parents wouldn't approve of her seeing a man fourteen years her senior, she told him to pick her up on Queensway, nearly two miles from her home. Not wishing to appear too pushy, she didn't bother to ask where they would be going; nor did she care, just so long as they were together.

When she spotted his car moving along the crowded street, Joan ran over and hopped in for what turned out to be a leisurely drive to Hanover Square, on the other side of Hyde Park. Surrounding a handsomely manicured acre of greenery, the square's old structures were among the stateliest in London, housing both quaint offices and much-in-demand apartments. When Reed pulled up in front of one such building, Joan glanced excitedly from her companion to the ornate bow windows and faded brick façade, expecting to be shown to a secret jive club the likes of which were only known to stars like Reed. Instead, after ascending to the building's penthouse, Joan found herself in Reed's opulent flat.

Suddenly Reed's halo lost some of its radiance. He had neither music nor dinner nor even a movie in mind: he'd apparently brought her to his apartment for sex.

Joan, who had rarely kept a boyfriend for more than a week, had never slept with any of them. Not that she was saving herself for marriage; she was willing to give herself fully in the name of love and/or romance. This was neither. In fact, the presumptuousness Reed had shown in bringing her to his flat

was a distinct turnoff. But before Joan could recover
from her shock and disappointment, she says that
Reed fed her a Mickey and, for the next few hours,
she slipped in and out of consciousness while he
raped her.

Reed has never given his side of the story, but
chances are good that Joan's version is close to the
truth. Contract stars of this era were fond of "scorekeeping," seeing how many studio actresses they
could bed just for the hell of it. Deflowering young
starlets was considered especially prestigious. It's
clear that Reed and Harvey had compared notes after
the party and, learning from his colleague that Joan
was a virgin, the more aggressive Reed had made it
his goal to take her. However, to stave off possible
rejection and subsequent loss of face, Reed had
stacked the deck—whether through a Mickey or by a
string of potent drinks is irrelevant. He had gotten
what he wanted and would be able to boast about it
the following day. Nor could Joan have defended her
unscrupulously stolen honor. If she were indiscreet
and complained about having been rendered insen-
sible, she'd have been labeled a bad sport. After all, if
she hadn't "wanted it," she wouldn't have gone with
Reed to his flat.

Joan regained her wits, at least, several hours later.
When she realized what had happened, she felt
cheap and abused; worse, when she saw that her
curfew of two o'clock had come and gone, she felt
even more awful. Not only would she have to lie to
her parents about where she'd been but she would
have to do so in as frayed an emotional state as she
had ever been.

She put herself together in a frantic state and Reed,
who was helpful, though likely smugly satisfied,
drove her home. She went in alone to find just what
she'd expected: her parents waiting up for her, Joe
livid with rage. Compounding the lateness of the
hour, Joan initially lied about where she'd been—to a

party with Laurence Harvey, she told them. But her parents had called Harvey, who said that she wasn't with him. Crying—nor was it an act; she was genuinely unsettled from the night's events—Joan covered that lie with another, claiming that she'd bumped into some friends from RADA and that they'd had an impromptu reunion. This satisfied her mother, who helped to pacify Joe. Snorting out the last of his rage, he forgave Joan and told her to go to bed. But Joan didn't even try to get much-needed sleep. She was due at the studio in just over two hours and, cleaning herself up, walked numbly to the tube station two blocks away for what proved an especially long train ride to Ealing.

When Reed phoned later in the day to ask Joan to dinner, she was astonished to find herself more pleased than angry. But the part of her that still seethed and hurt was also a slave to reality, and the reality she accepted was that she couldn't go backward in time. The only way to regain her self-respect was to try to create a relationship ex post facto, allowing the aberration of the night before to be written off as "enthusiasm." She was happy, too, because he wasn't discarding her like a used tissue, nor was he out simply for sex, which she'd have denied him in any case. For Joan, the call represented a much-needed step back toward respectability, and she embraced it.

On that night and on the dates that followed, Reed was not only well behaved but usually enchanting. He had the mood swings of any actor—so did Joan, for that matter—and sometimes, when he was with his friends, he would get a little rowdy and discourteous. But no one was perfect, Joan rationalized, and most of the time they enjoyed each other's company. Joan was still star-struck and was happy to be seen about town with Reed. She still, however, had some Victorian ideas about relationships which forced her to take a lot of guff. "I'm a completely old-fashioned girl," she boasted. "I don't think females are equal to males. Man is superior, stronger physically, more intellectual, more logical. And I'm jolly glad. I don't want to be independent and make decisions."

For his part, Reed obviously liked having a beautiful and vivacious starlet on his arm, especially one who adored him. Then too, Britain's up-and-coming "bad girl" had a way of getting photographed when she went out—exposure which couldn't hurt his career. Not so coincidentally, after making thirteen films in succession, *Flame of Araby* was the only picture Reed had out in 1952—this at a time when contract players were doing three and four movies a year. Which is not to say that Reed was only being opportunistic by latching onto Joan's rising star. As he later confessed in a moment of uncharacteristic frankness, "She was the only girl I ever fell in love with." But their relationship *did* have its practical side.

After several dates, Joan was sleeping with Reed again, this time of her own volition. However, the emotional scar tissue of their infamous first date prevented her from ever fully enjoying the experience, though she didn't realize it at the time. Although her mother had never talked about sex, Elsa was constantly catering to Joe, leading Joan to deduce that sex was a chore for women to grin and bear.

Despite her general satisfaction with the relationship, Joan resisted the suggestion Reed made after several weeks that she live with him. Joan couldn't do that to her parents and she wasn't sure she wanted to do that to herself. Reed had a philosophy about actresses which frightened her: he felt they were over the hill once they hit their mid-twenties. He had often said as much about Joan. "He told me I had better get all the work I could because by the time I was twenty-three I would be too old." She didn't want to move in with him only to be shown the door in a few years because she was nearing the quarter-century mark.

Rebuffed, Reed let the subject sit for a while. Then, in April, he broached the idea of marriage. This was more to Joan's liking, since she honestly believed that marriage was forever, and she urged him to ask her parents for her hand. The notion struck Reed as hopelessly old-fashioned but it appealed to the actor in him. He would get to play a romantic lead for a small but *very* interested audience. Beaming, Joan set up a dinner at Harley House, after which Reed put on his brightest smile and, asking for their blessing, won Elsa's heart. Joe, however, was far from moved. Being in the business, he was not unaware of Reed's playboy reputation. He was also uneasy about the age difference between his daughter and Reed, not just the fourteen years that separated them but the fact that Joan was still only eighteen. But she was a feisty eighteen, and when Reed's deepest dimples failed to persuade Joe, Joan played her trump card. If her parents didn't grant their approval, they would live together. Joe wasn't the kind of father who bowed to extortion, but Elsa was shocked and scared.

A halt was called to the discussion, and Reed left. For the rest of the night, and for several nights thereafter, the debate raged on. Elsa had already resolved to give in if she could convince Joe. "Other girls become brides in their teens and make their marriages successful," she said she told herself. "Perhaps Joan and Max would stand a chance after all." But Joe refused to budge, Elsa recalling that he said over and over, "She's too young to know her own mind."

The night it finally came to a head was the worst of them all. "Joan's father was adamant," Elsa remembered. "He stormed one night after reasoning had failed, 'If you marry that man I shall never speak to you again.' Then he stalked out." Joan started to cry and, said Elsa, "When he returned several hours later, Joan was still in tears." Those tears were what finally softened him. Entering the room, he looked down at his daughter and sat beside her. Putting his arm around her, he said quietly, "All right, all right," and reluctantly gave her his permission to wed. Just *how* reluctantly was made clear by what he said next—that he would disown Joan if the marriage didn't work out.

It wasn't exactly a vote of confidence, but Joan had long ago stopped expecting what she wanted or needed from her father. In any case, from here on her parents would be a secondary influence in her life. What mattered most to her would be her husband and her budding career at Rank.

Chapter Five

◆◆◆◆◆◆◆◆◆◆◆◆◆◆◆◆◆◆◆◆◆◆◆◆◆◆◆◆◆◆◆◆◆◆◆

The couple were married on Saturday, May 24, 1952, a day after Joan's nineteenth birthday. For days before she had gone through the periods of doubt suffered by many brides-to-be, exacerbated by the feeling that she was living under the media's magnifying glass. Indeed, when it came time to tie the knot at Caxton Hall in London (where, coincidentally, divorces were also granted), the photographers and journalists all but outnumbered the guests. But Joan was tailor-made for the tabloids—a beautiful starlet, just signed to a contract with Rank, taking a stunning film star as her husband. Both Reed and her father advised her that she would have to get used to it.

The Reeds honeymooned in the South of France,

where Joan was her typical outgoing self, and for the first time Reed became uneasy when she talked to men; he was particularly bothered when she was photographed alone. In fairness to Reed, he was experienced enough with the press to know that innocent activities could be distorted and he didn't want some casual event to cause stories back in London such as: "Is Joan's marriage over? The sexy 'bad girl' was caught by our photographer making eyes at a handsome lifeguard. . . ." On the other hand, Reed was discouraged at not having any work, and that caused him to overreact. Not that he needed to act in the same sense that Joan did: Maxwell Reed wasn't an artist so much as a salesman. Whether he was selling audiences a character on the screen or pitching himself as a prospective son-in-law, he was happiest when wheeling and dealing; the bigger the stakes, the happier he was.

But he couldn't bear inactivity, and he took it out on Joan. To make matters worse, she had to start a film a few days hence: *Decameron Nights*. That didn't make him jealous, for he'd been in business long enough to realize, as he put it, "All actors have their ups and downs." However, it did leave him frustrated because there was no one with whom to commiserate, no kindred show biz victim. Thus, when they were alone in France he made her into a victim—*his* victim. First he'd yell at her, and if Joan in her independent way stood up to him, he'd become physical. She wouldn't provoke him intentionally, but in his state of mind every contrary opinion was a deep affront and he'd respond by grabbing his wife hard, throttling her, and even smacking her.

Because Reed didn't know how to control himself or even how to apologize, it took just a few days for Joan to feel utterly alone. Rather than create problems, Joan said as little as possible and managed to ride it out to the weekend, when she had to leave to work on *Decameron Nights*. Ironically, their last day in

France was the most pleasant of the honeymoon, for a millionaire had recognized Reed and broached the idea of making movies—a chance for the actor to boast, to wheedle, to charm, and to sell. In fact, Reed had such a good time with the fellow that he decided to stay in France to try to put together some kind of independent deal. It was a long shot, one that ultimately didn't pan out, but Joan didn't care. If it lifted Reed out of his depression, she wanted him to stay.

Upset, but hopeful that Reed's mood was a passing phase, Joan flew to Madrid, where *Decameron Nights* was being shot. It was a minor role for her, playing, in her words, "a mischievous minx of a lady-in-waiting," and she began to look forward to Reed's arrival the following week, hoping they could get out and see some of the Spanish countryside. But Reed came to Spain in a foul humor. His millionaire had left him without any kind of commitment, and the buzz of activity on the film set only served to whet Reed's appetite. Almost at once he was angry and lashed out, and because Joan couldn't strike back without Reed resorting to violence, she took out her dander on the film. She says, "I ignored attempts to discipline me," and remembers becoming so annoyed with life that she intentionally went out in "tight jeans [and] was almost arrested for wearing them on the street." Back on the soundstage, she complained about everyone from the costumer to the director—and this was just the *first* film of her Rank contract; Joan hadn't even started making the tiresome string of teen melodramas.

After her stint in *Decameron Nights*, Joan hurried back to England to start on *The Cosh Boy*. Luckily, Reed also got in a film, playing a smuggler in *Sea Devils*, so he was in relatively high spirits. Then Rank gave them both parts in Basil Dearden's boxing film, *The Square Ring*, which, as it turned out, was to be the last good role Reed would ever have. All the while their relationship was not only tolerable but often pleasurable. They bought a boat and spent the weekends sailing and generally having a good time, and it's safe to assume that Joan wanted Reed's career to stay on track even more than did Reed himself!

To this end, since Rank had nothing for either actor after *The Square Ring*, they decided to do a play. They had acted together before on the stage, spending a week in *The Seventh Veil* just prior to their marriage, and now they undertook a limited engagement of *The Skin of Our Teeth*, a Pulitzer Prize-winning play by Thorton Wilder. Joan played the maid Sabina, a temptress in the household of George Antrobus (Reed) in this metaphorical study of man against the world down through the ages. Much to her utter delight, Joan had the last laugh on RADA by getting a world-class play *because* she was a popular film star and, to top it all off, earning superb notices for her efforts.

After *The Skin of Our Teeth*, Joan was caught up in her miserable "bad girl" stage and Reed was unemployed. Rather than spend his days, as he describes it, "sitting around the flat eating and sleeping and painting," he began actively soliciting work. Few undertakings are more difficult or more demeaning in the film business than knocking on doors, since producers are reluctant to hire anyone who must resort to selling himself. But Reed couldn't just sit around, if for no other reason that that he didn't want to become known as "Mr. Collins." He put out feelers that extended all the way to Rome, where Reed was popular and keenly wanted to go—not merely for the work but because there was "lots of lolly" (money) and plenty of sun. He went to meetings, met with producers, and talked himself up; yet for all his charm and savvy, he failed to land a single job.

After months of being idle and putting on a happy front for the public while he battled with Joan in private, Reed concluded that the only way to rekindle his fast-fading career was to move to Southern California. While the advent of television hurt the film business there as well, Hollywood had responded by devising a slew of gimmicks to lure people back into the theaters, from Cinerama to 3-D to Smell-O-Vision, and by mounting mammoth pictures like *Samson and Delilah* and *Quo Vadis*, which dwarfed anything the home screen could offer. Thus, filmmaking continued apace. Even so, if he couldn't beat TV he could always join it by doing a series.

For her part, Joan was not at all unreceptive to the idea of going to Hollywood. It might solve the problem of Reed's increasingly volatile nature and would free her from Rank and typecasting. She had come to accept the fact that for all her protests, "[Rank] was going to go on casting me as bad girls till the cows came home," and though she didn't agree with her husband's idea that actresses were over the hill at twenty-three, she realized that "if a girl doesn't reach the absolute topnotch [roles] in two years, she's through. They type you by that time." She saw Hollywood as a way out, if for no other reason than that the British studios "don't bother to build women up. They concentrate on building up the men."

Unfortunately, Joan happened to do some complaining in an interview and drew the wrath of local tabloids, to wit Donald Zec of the *Daily Mirror* who wrote; "If she takes my advice she will turn her back on California—and concentrate on Kew [i.e. the stage]. She will learn a little more about the art of acting; of growing up . . . and," he concluded with his sharpest barb, "how to scratch along contentedly on a hundred quid a week."

Not surprisingly, Joan couldn't have cared less about the reporter's advice. However, much to her delight she *did* get a reprieve from the femme fatale roles, being cast as a precocious teenager in the comedy *Our Girl Friday* (released in the U.S. as *The Adventures of Sadie*). Although she knew she'd been given the part because of her body and not her talent—"I wore a bikini to provide the sex appeal," she admits—the part allowed her to do movie comedy, a field she wanted to conquer even more than the stage. "I see myself as the second coming of Carole Lombard," she said, adding that she wanted nothing more than to continue doing "light comedy sort of thing. That's what I'm best at." But *Our Girl Friday* proved to be a fluke, for she would soon be back in form giving birth out of wedlock in *The Good Die Young*.

By February 1954, Joan was at a professional and personal nadir. Reed was spending a lot of time in Rome, but when he was home it was hell. Professionally she had no films pending—a mixed blessing, given her feeling about the roles she'd been playing. Joan went so far as to screen-test for parts that were out of character for her, but no matter how well she did Rank wanted her just where they had her: bringing in hundreds of thousands of dollars by playing naughty and/or scantily clad women, or being loaned out to *other* studios to make films about naughty and/or scantily clad women.

As much to get away from Reed as to challenge herself creatively, Joan signed on to do another play, one that would tour England. The vehicle was *The Praying Mantis*, and although she was playing yet another vamp, she felt more fulfilled doing it on the stage. She was on the road for a month, earning some $20 a week on top of her Rank salary, and when she returned to the Hanover Square apartment she was so euphoric about the stage that she began preparing for another play while awaiting word about film properties.

The reason for her joy was twofold. During her four weeks on tour, Joan had not only put some distance between herself and her husband, giving her some emotional peace, but she'd been hanging out with working actors. The old Slob came creeping back, the feeling of the stage as actor's country, the joy of not having to do retakes or perform in bits and pieces as in film, the gratification of having a live audience to play to, the thrill of discovering something new about a character each night. Of course, Reed hadn't been a part of Joan's life during her RADA days, so he seemed strangely out of place when she returned. But his intemperate behavior brought her back to earth and, compared to the month she'd just spent in heaven, it was a place she was beginning to like less and less.

When Reed suggested one night that they go to dinner at the chic Les Ambassadeurs, Joan hurriedly seconded the motion. She didn't enjoy staying home for dinner, since she didn't like to cook. Moreover, Reed usually didn't like what she cooked and would refuse to eat it. "I am very good at simple things," Joan conceded, "for example salads, but I hate the preparing and washing up." By going to Les Ambassadeurs, Joan would make her husband happy by giving him the opportunity to do some huckstering as well as giving her a night out. The nightclub was a haven for visiting film luminaries and the rich and successful from other walks of life. Even if Reed didn't have a prayer of striking a deal, at least he could prowl and mingle and feel as though he were doing something useful.

The crowd was the usual glittering, lively group that night, and Joan enjoyed having a few drinks, listening to the live band, and watching the patrons as they danced.

After he had been gone for quite a while, Reed suddenly returned to where Joan was seated, and with a curious grin pulled her onto the dance floor. They were quiet for a moment, after which he told her that there was a man at the nightclub, an Arab sheik, who had recognized Joan and offered him over $20,000 to sleep with her just one night.

Joan wasn't sure Reed was serious and said nothing. Then, though obviously torn himself, Reed suggested to his wife that it might not be a bad idea to consider the offer.

Now that she knew he wasn't kidding, Joan's expression quickly shaded from calm to anger. She began to yell at Reed who, glowering down at her, cut the tirade short by reminding her that with that much money they could move to Hollywood. Hearing his practical attitude toward the sale of her body, Joan became positively hysterical. She cried and shouted even louder, not caring a damn about Hollywood or Reed or the people around them, wishing only that the earth would swallow up her husband and his compulsion for deal-making.

The festivities at Les Ambassadeurs slogged to an embarrassed standstill at Joan's flare-up, with all eyes upon her. She flung a final oath at Reed, who stood there fuming and mortified, then, turning, she stormed through the nightclub and took a taxi to Harley House. As far as she was concerned, the next deal she wanted to hear of involving Reed was his own divorce. And she resolved that if anyone *else* tried to hurt her, whether it was her father because she'd ended the marriage, or Rank because of her growing disgust with *that* relationship, she'd spit in his eye as well.

No one, she vowed, would ever again try to stick *anything* to Joan Collins.

Chapter Six

◆◆◆◆◆◆◆◆◆◆◆◆◆◆◆◆◆◆◆◆◆◆◆◆◆◆◆◆◆◆◆◆◆◆◆◆◆◆◆

To Joan's relief, the threatened repercussions did not materialize on the home front, and she once again started living with her family. According to Elsa, all she and her father ever said regarding the episode was the following exchange, prompted by Joan: "You were right, I should have listened to you," to which Joe replied unhappily, "Why does this have to be the one time in my life that I've been able to say, 'I told you so'?"

The matter was closed, and though it's fair to say her father had mellowed in two years, his changed attitude was also due to Joan's own growth. "I don't regret the marriage," she told a reporter at the time. "It taught me some valuable lessons—in particular, to curb my impulsiveness and not to expect life to be a make-believe fairy tale." Joan may have lost some virtue in her father's eyes, but she had replaced it with newfound confidence and maturity.

Reed, however, was less satisfied with the way things had worked out. For one thing, her departure had left him hurting financially. He said at the time, "I've got enough cash to stop me from starving," but that was literally about all he had. He couldn't even get to the money in their joint account, complaining, "I have asked her to countersign checks so I can draw some money out of it, but she stops them." Still, what hurt more was the very fact that she was gone. For all his flaws, eccentricities, and ego Reed *did* care for Joan, and he felt lost with neither a wife nor a

44

career of which to speak. Some months after they were legally separated he admitted, "I am still in love with her."

At the moment, all he could do was lick his wounds and concentrate on finding work. However, in the months that followed, he and Joan discovered that while they'd gone their separate ways, they were bound by an emotional tether which, on two different occasions, would snap them back together with cataclysmic results.

Joan neither missed Reed nor had the time or inclination to look back on their failed marriage. She started seeing other men, including actors like the late Robert Quarry, though she was much more discriminating than she'd been before. She'd go out a great deal, but if a man didn't treat her "with respect or consideration," she wouldn't see him again. Having endured the caprice and frequent discourtesy of Reed, Joan had developed "the utmost respect for myself, and any man who does not feel the same about me is a nonstarter."

Before long Marylebone Road was littered with corpses, for while Joan was busy raising her standards, she was finding out that most men couldn't meet them. "Englishmen don't really like women," she concluded. "I've seen it in my father and in every other Englishman I've ever known. There's an in-built coldness there that they simply cannot help. They'd much rather be out drinking with the boys or watching football in the rain than having a candlelit dinner for two with a girl." Years later, after going through therapy, Joan would modify her standards by admitting that *some* of her dissatisfaction with men was her own fault, "subconsciously expecting rejection from men" because of Reed, and making sure that she was the one who struck first. Back in mid-1954, however, she was anxious to show men, her family, and herself that she was a class act.

Because English studios as well as Englishmen were déclassé as far as Joan was concerned, it was a stroke of good luck that Hollywood came calling. Several months earlier, Joan had gone to Paris to screen-test for director Howard Hawks, who was making *Gentlemen Prefer Blondes*. She wasn't selected for that film, but Hawks was sufficiently impressed that when he was looking for someone to star with Jack Hawkins and James Robertson Justice in the quasi-Biblical epic *Land of the Pharaohs*, he gave her a call. "Be in Rome in three days," the veteran director ordered. "I'm not even going to test you for the role of Nellifer."

Though Joan was busy preparing another play, she dropped it and took the next plane to Rome. Hawks was the big time, the man who had directed Gary Cooper in *Sergeant York*, Katharine Hepburn and Cary Grant in *Bringing Up Baby*, Bogart and Bacall in *To Have and Have Not*. He was a starmaker, and Joan badly wanted to be a star. For its part, Rank was happy to loan her to Warner Brothers. Not only would they collect tens of thousands of dollars while continuing to pay her her low contractual wages, but if she *did* become a star it would mean bigger box-office returns for any film they made with her.

Just then, however, Joan didn't care about money, contracts, or studios. One of the world's great directors wanted her to star in a major film, and that was all that mattered. Yet, between her arrival in Rome and the day the cameras started rolling, something happened to Joan which jeopardized not merely *Land of the Pharaohs* but her career itself: she fell in love with her co-star.

Sydney Chaplin, age twenty-eight, was the second son of comic Charlie Chaplin and actress Lita Grey. Tall and slender, he had his father's sparkling eyes and the Cheshire smile of one who was perched on a high limb, content to watch everyone else go mad while he enjoyed his life. A Hollywood brat, Chaplin was a hedonist who didn't care very much for acting and wasn't particularly good at it. After training at the Circle Theater in Los Angeles, he made his first movie in 1952, when his father cast him in *Limelight*; it was two years before he made his next movie, playing a thief in a minor British film called *Confession* (released in the U.S. as *The Deadliest Sin*). *Land of the Pharaohs* was his third movie, and he was featured as Nellifer's lover.

Because he received money regularly from his father, Sydney didn't have to work steadily. Thus, in a quarter-century of making movies, he appeared in a mere eleven, two of which were for his father and the rest of which were largely insignificant. He was somewhat more enamored with Broadway and enjoyed doing musicals like *Subways Are for Sleeping* and *Funny Girl*, where his flamboyant, devil-may-care manner was more appropriate. It's also likely that since his father did not act on the stage, Sydney felt less intimidated in treading the boards.

To say that Joan was ripe for the breezy Chaplin is an understatement. He wasn't English, his career didn't matter nearly as much as having a good time, and he had a quality which Joan admired above all others: a sense of humor. "That," she said, "is what I look for in a man." After having been the uptight Mrs. Reed, she was ready to break out. The problem was that Joan still hadn't learned how to do anything in moderation.

She and Chaplin quickly became lovers, sharing laughter, late hours, and an excess of food and drink. As in Spain, Joan embraced the immoderate and became a problem to the filmmakers and natives alike—although this time it wasn't defiance but the example of Chaplin's dauntless joie de vivre that spurred her on. "I wore the first bikini seen locally," she remembers, creating quite a stir at the beach; and it didn't matter, she said, that "I knew I was wrong."

She amused Chaplin and he encouraged her, which was all the motivation she needed.

Hawks was understandably annoyed by these shenanigans, since they had a way of spilling over onto his movie. One of the biggest problems was that Joan's nights out at fancy restaurants caused her to put on weight. "I've never worn less in a film," she says, "spangled bras, shredded silver skirts, bangles on my wrists, and a jeweled ruby in my navel," and it was not a wardrobe sympathetic to so much as a single added pound. The late hours also made it difficult for Joan to study her lines, let alone remember them, and she had trouble even taking the picture seriously when Chaplin was around. Though Joan was equally at home in modern or period pieces, Chaplin's bemused attitude toward the exotic costumes and stilted, mock-classical dialogue of *Land of the Pharaohs* prevented her from working diligently.

Hawks was constantly chastising them both, though only Joan took it to heart. She'd try to behave for a while, but there was always the siren call of Mr. Chaplin to draw her to wine, fast cars, and sex. And then there was the unexpected return of Maxwell Reed. Both were a distraction, but if Chaplin's presence was like a feather tickling her body, Reed's appearance in Rome was like a lead pipe coming down hard across the back of her neck.

By extraordinary coincidence, Reed was also at the Cinecittà studios, playing a small role in *Helen of Troy*, which was to be his last film. Before coming over, he had written to Joan and though he says, "She never answered any of my letters," he hoped he would be able to see her in Rome. When they did finally meet, Reed says it was by chance. "One day I saw her on the beach with some men friends. I went over to speak to her, but she screamed at me to go away, saying that we were through. It was a terrible scene."

According to Joan, the meeting was far from innocent. He had come, she says, to blackmail her by using nude photos he had taken when they were married. If she didn't buy the pictures back, he would sell them to a magazine that offered a great deal of money for the shots. Fearful of the impact the topless photos would have on her career, Joan maintains that she agreed to his terms, which included cash and jewelry, but never received the photos, as Reed had promised. Nor, it should be mentioned, did they ever appear in print.

As in so many of the events which involved Joan and Reed and no one else, the truth seems to lie somewhere between what each of them claims. Reed *had* gone looking for her, but only because she had refused to give him access to money he desperately needed. He had reminded her of his quandary in the letters, and when she greeted him on the beach with a bitchy cold shoulder—Joan acknowledges that the men she was with actually tried to chase him away— the superhuckster in Reed came vaulting to his rescue with the gambit involving the photos. It was neither a tactful nor a loving ploy, but it *was* an effective alternative to diplomacy.

Regardless of how the encounter evolved, it left Joan shaken and preoccupied which, on top of the problems she was already having on *Land of the Pharaohs*, was the last thing she needed. Yet, in a way, it was a good thing to have happened, for she realized that she had to get a grip on herself and was much more conscientious about her work throughout the remainder of production.

As it turned out, Joan could have spared herself the effort. Despite a literate script co-authored by William Faulkner, of all people, this saga of the Fourth Dynasty Pharaoh Khufu is as plodding an epic as ever reached the screen. Even Collins's passionate scenes with the horribly miscast Chaplin aren't enough to relieve the boredom of what is widely considered to be Hawks's worst film.

However, all was not lost for Joan. During the course of shooting, the set had been visited by one of the most powerful men in Hollywood—Darryl F. Zanuck, head of production at 20th Century-Fox. At the time, Zanuck happened to be a very *annoyed* head of production, having just learned that his biggest star, Marilyn Monroe, had quit the studio for a second time. Sick of her antics, he began to think about grooming a replacement—and when he saw Joan he believed she could fill her shoes, among other things. "That girl acts with the authority of a bull-whip," the legendary mogul told an assistant, adding that he was even more impressed with her "face and chassis."

As soon as he returned to Hollywood, Zanuck looked at some of the other work Joan had done and was convinced he'd found the next Monroe. Contacting Rank, he offered to buy the remainder of her contract outright for £15,000. They accepted and Joan, now back in London, was offered $350 a week to make movies for Fox. However, as much as she wanted to go to Hollywood, Joan resented being sold "like a side of beef," and was particularly unhappy with the salary. Not that she was greedy: she simply realized that Zanuck's enthusiasm for her could wane, in which case she'd be trapped in nothing but little films for the duration of her seven-year pact. The only way of assuring herself topnotch films was to transform herself from the new kid on the block into a very expensive piece of overhead. That way, the studio would have to use her in big movies to justify her cost.

"I had heard stories about how it pays to be firm out there from the start," she says. "You don't just accept things or show gratitude—that's fatal. You tell them you want this and that." She did, making her demands to John Shepbridge of the Famous Artists Agency, who was handling the deal. She told the disbelieving agent that she wanted $1,250 a week, a contract which lasted only two years, and various perks. Shepbridge raged at what he could only chalk up to sheer insanity on her part, but Joan was adamant. Shepbridge agreed to relay her "request" to Fox, and Joan left his office in an uncharacteristic state of serenity and contentment. If she lost Hollywood, she would fly to Paris to be with Chaplin; if Zanuck acquiesced, she would be on her way to certain superstardom. For once, whatever happened, Joan Collins felt she would be a winner.

As it turned out, Zanuck acquiesced. And Joan, filled with a renewed sense of worth and confidence, promptly flew to Paris to celebrate. It was, however, the last time she would ever have her cake and eat it too.

Chapter Seven

◆◆

Joan went to Hollywood in the closing weeks of 1954, her high hopes soured only by the fact that she'd miss her family, friends, and homeland. But she'd get to meet and work with the most famous stars in the world and she knew that, in time, she would make new friends. And she'd be away from the British press, whose hostility had reached new heights in its coverage of her departure for the U.S., with comments like, "She wasn't made up at all and looked terrible. . . ." It wasn't exactly a wash, the loss, she felt, outweighed the gain, since she was closer to her family than she'd ever been. But it was the only way to achieve the kind of stardom she used to dream about, and she would have something else that mattered a great deal: financial independence. She'd be starting with Fox at a salary of $65,000 a year, which wasn't bad for a twenty-one-year-old. In addition, the studio had agreed to foot the bill for at least one trip to England each year, which, she told her proud but heartbroken mother, would be upon them before they knew it.

After arriving in Hollywood, Joan took a small apartment in the Beverly Carlton on Olympic Boulevard in Beverly Hills, and plunged into two projects which kept her busy round the clock: helping the publicity mill at Fox promote her, and preparing for her Hollywood film debut opposite none other than Bette Davis in *The Virgin Queen*.

The studio publicists did a superb job of getting Joan's picture into papers and magazines nationwide. From 1955 to 1957 she seemed to be everywhere—showing a bit of leg to pilots at the airport, playing golf with Ben Hogan to stay in shape (though she didn't know the first thing about the game), staring pensively into a fake studio fireplace. She appeared over and over in all the movie magazines, was featured in *Life*, the *Saturday Evening Post*, and other mainstream publications, and found herself interviewed for more newspaper columns than she ever knew existed. And while a great deal of this coverage was due to the influence of Zanuck and Fox, a lot of it was also the result of Joan's own innate appeal. As columnist Earl Wilson gushed at the time, "She's the zippiest, unstuffiest British actress we know," a sentiment echoed by Louella Parsons, who wrote, "I don't see how anybody could be bored with Joan Collins."

Concurrently, Joan was preparing for *The Virgin Queen*, in which she'd be playing a love of Sir Walter Raleigh—a girl who, as fate would have it, ends up an unwed mother. But this was not like the films Joan had done for Rank, and she worked hard learning the part, not to mention spending hour upon hour being fitted for the colorful Elizabethan costumes.

Despite her boundless energy, all of this activity left Joan exhausted. After several weeks, she still felt like an outsider. She had her boosters, of course, among them fellow contract player Sheree North. "I liked her on sight," says North. "She had a spirit of independence and a quiet air of 'If you like me fine, but if you don't I won't cry about it.' She wasn't going to be bothered trying to meet and ingratiate herself with the top VIPs as so many newcomers do." But if Joan wouldn't cry in public, she did shed more than a few tears in private. In her weary state she began to take her alienation personally, nor was she being unusually paranoid. While many of the people at Fox worked hard to make her feel welcome, others treated her like "a commodity" rather than as a serious actress. "People automatically assumed I was a 'dumb broad,' and they treated me like one," she says, something which was dramatically underscored at one of the first Hollywood parties she attended.

"I was introduced to Frank Sinatra," she recalls, "who was dressed just like a Damon Runyon character, and I told him I thought he looked as though he had just stepped out of *Guys and Dolls*. Well, Humphrey Bogart was standing next to us and he turned on me, grabbed hold of the front of my dress, pulled me toward him and said, 'Don't you *ever* talk about a pal of mine like that.' He was furious and treated me like one of the molls in his films. I'm sure if I'd have been plain and unattractive he would have behaved differently. But then, I suppose if I'd have been plain and unattractive, I wouldn't have been invited to the party at all." Joan wasn't supposed to have an opinion, and if she did she was to keep it to herself. "I was nothing more than a decoration," she reports, "and this, of course, was humiliating."

Equally embarrassing was the discrimination she felt when she went to a party. Preceded by her sexpot, mankiller image, she says that when she'd start talking to "someone's husband, it's odds on that his wife would come and drag him away."

She shied away from parties after those experiences and, as a consequence, got to know very few people. Nor were there any jazz clubs like she'd known in London, or parks where she could go for a walk. She kept busy writing countless letters to England, especially to teenager Jackie—the future author of *Hollywood Wives*—who, prophetically, had specifically asked to be kept abreast of all the latest gossip from Hollywood. But staying at home made Joan stir crazy, and she realized that for all it had to offer an actor, Hollywood had very little for a human being: it was clannish and sterile. Even the much-vaunted stars had failed to impress her. In addition to Bogart and Sinatra, she'd met Clark Gable and Marlon Brando, saying of the first that "he didn't send me at all," and of the latter that he was "nothing sensational."

"I was miserable," she sums it all up. "I hated not only the town but every single inhabitant, including every single geranium." Finally, after being molested by a man while she was walking one night, Joan realized she had to get away, if for no other reason than to keep *The Virgin Queen* from becoming a valve for the pressure building inside of her. So Joan hopped on a plane and flew to Paris—right into the arms of Sydney Chaplin.

"On the way, I ran into weather difficulties," she remembers. "There was a storm, but the combination of Paris, my favorite city, and Syd, my favorite person at the time, was irresistible. It was foggy, cold, and rainy all the time I was in Paris, but I never even noticed it. I forgot all about Hollywood and my career. I had a beautiful time there."

It was a beautiful time for Chaplin as well, and when it came time for Joan to leave for *The Virgin Queen*, they discussed the idea of Chaplin going with her. Though he couldn't up and leave without cleaning up some personal matters, there was nothing tying him to Paris permanently. Thus, he agreed to follow Joan over within a week or two. Joan was ecstatic, and upon her return wasn't surprised to find that Hollywood didn't look quite as dreary as when she'd left.

The Virgin Queen was made primarily to give Bette

Davis a second crack at playing Queen Elizabeth. The first time she'd done the part was in 1939 in *The Private Lives of Elizabeth and Essex*. Davis had wanted Laurence Olivier to play her lover Essex. Instead, Warner Brothers had given her the debonair but less gifted Errol Flynn. That spoiled the film and colored Davis's performance, and she yearned to do it again. This time, instead of Essex, Elizabeth had to deal with the two-timing Raleigh in the person of Richard Todd.

Throughout her long career, Bette Davis was effusive with praise, brusque and frequently loud with criticism, and rarely without one or the other on her tongue. On those few occasions when she didn't have an answer, she would turn the spotlight on someone else, exclaim, "You're brilliant, *you* tell them!" and, often grinning, wait impatiently for an answer.

One of Davis's most deeply held convictions was that movie stars are American royalty who should strive to be glamourous offscreen as well as on. However, being a petite five foot one, and remembered more for her talent than for her build or beauty, the actress *did* tend to run bosomy newcomers through the mill:

Enter Joan Collins.

As far as Davis was concerned, Joan was just one of several saviors-in-training being primed to replace Monroe if need be, others including Jayne Mansfield and Sheree North. What's more, Joan's offscreen style, while acceptable for the fifties, was not exactly Bette's idea of glamour: as Joan describes it, "a black dress slit to the instep and hair hanging over my face [and] bop talk"—not to mention the matching gold nail polish and sandals of which she was fond.

Two years later, Joan would look back on her first months in Hollywood and say, "I used to have the most atrocious taste in clothes and makeup of anybody in Hollywood. I always used to bop in front of them, so they treated me like a crazy kid." Not unexpectedly, the crusty Davis was one of the first to do just that. An expert on the Elizabethan era, she jumped on gestures or enunciation that were anachronistic, sometimes making her suggestions through the director, other times not. She had no patience when lines were muffed or, more subjectively, when she failed to see passion or anger or the kind of emotion *she* wanted to see in Joan's eyes. This, coupled with her distrust of any actress who stood five foot five and a half, measured 38–23–37, and had the face of an angel, made Joan an easy target.

Although Joan wisely avoided Davis whenever possible, she was at her mercy for the several months the cameras were rolling. A pity, since Joan wasn't as shoddy an individual or as sloppy an actress as Davis seemed to think and, had Joan gotten closer to her, Davis could have taught her a great deal about screen acting. But they took their roles as queen and lady-in-waiting to heart, which proved a detriment to them both.

Chaplin's arrival during the shoot boosted Joan's spirits, distracted her on occasion, and made Hollywood more bearable—for a while. After moving into the $250-a-month apartment she'd taken on Beverly Glen Boulevard in Westwood, he remembered just why he didn't spend a lot of time in his native Southern California: there wasn't very much to do. Unlike other major cities, Los Angeles was essentially a film town. If one was not a part of that social whirl, making deals at parties, chatting with columnists over lunch, or talking up clients or scripts over dinner, one was an outsider. It was the perfect environment for a Maxwell Reed, but not for Joan or the expatriate Chaplin.

Although there were frequent engagements with friends like the Gene Kellys and producer George Englund and his wife Cloris Leachman, Joan still felt displaced and Chaplin quickly grew to miss the character to be found in cities like Paris and London, where he'd spent time with Joan after *Land of the Pharaohs*. He became bored, which spoiled his good humor; since they were living together, that brought Joan down as well. She didn't have much time to brood about it, because no sooner was *The Virgin Queen* in the can than Marilyn Monroe refused to star in *The Girl in the Red Velvet Swing* and Joan got the plum part. While she went to work, Chaplin merely languished, his situation becoming a powder keg which needed only a spark to touch it off. . . .

The Girl in the Red Velvet Swing, from the Charles Samuels novel, was based on the true story of early twentieth-century showgirl Evelyn Nesbit, who had an affair with architect Stanford White while she was married to millionaire Harry K. Thaw. When Thaw found out, he fired three bullets into White's face and chest, killing him, and launching one of the most scandalous trials of the century. (Thaw was eventually acquitted by virtue of insanity and sent to the Matteawan asylum. Tellingly, after his release, he was tossed back in for sexually assaulting a nineteen-year-old boy). Ray Milland was selected to star as the doomed White, Thaw was given to Farley Granger, and Joan got to play her first American.

Topping it all off, once shooting began, Joan learned that the seventy-year-old Nesbit had been paid $45,000 to serve as a consultant, and would be coming around to answer any questions Joan might have as well as to watch the filming. Despite the creative dividends of being able to talk to the woman she was playing, Joan was terribly insecure lest she fail to impress her. However, her fears proved unfounded, Nesbit setting the stage by stating upon meeting Joan, "My, but you're lovely. How I envy your youth!," to which Joan replied that, to the contrary, she found it infinitely "more interesting to be getting older." That was actually the kindest thing

Joan could think to say, since Nesbit was fond of the
bottle and had drunk herself into a state of extraordinary disrepair. Joan was courteous to Nesbit throughout the shoot, but she found it difficult to admire this
shell of a once-vital woman.

The Girl in the Red Velvet Swing was a first-class
production, Fox shooting it in CinemaScope and
spending $1.6 million on a lavish production. How-
ever, if the film was Joan's professional high point,
that same period marked another low in her personal
life.

Chaplin's ennui had continued and, by the end of
the summer, not only wasn't he any fun but he was
proving eminently unsuitable for Joan. Jokes and
bawdy tales were his forte, not conversation, and
Joan badly needed to talk; going out in Hollywood
held no fascination for him, but sitting home watching TV or playing games was not for Joan. It all came
to a head while *The Girl in the Red Velvet Swing* was in
production. They had gone to Palm Springs for a
weekend respite, but it turned out to be the pro-
verbial last straw when Joan found Chaplin holding
court at the bar instead of spending time with her.
She started yelling at him, he yelled back, and the
relationship between the overworked actress and her
underworked lover came to an end.

Since Joan had never liked the furnished Beverly
Glen apartment, the parting with Chaplin was an
ideal time to leave it. She moved to West Hollywood,
taking an apartment in a large building on Olive
Drive, which slopes sharply from Sunset Boulevard
to the smoggy depths of Los Angeles. One thing that
appealed to her about the place was its proximity to
the clubs on the Strip, which were brimming with
vitality day and night. More important, however, was
that right across Sunset lay Miller Drive. One of the
narrowest, most winding streets in town, Miller was
where Arthur Loew, Jr., made his home. Never one
to waste time mourning a man, no sooner had the

actress parted company with Chaplin than she threw herself wholeheartedly into a relationship with their mutual friend and confidant, Loew. In many ways, it was to prove her most satisfying and successful relationship.

The polished and angular Loew was the grandson of Marcus Loew who, in 1924, had bought heavily into both Louis B. Mayer Pictures and the Goldwyn Company and merged them with his Metro Pictures to form Metro-Goldwyn-Mayer. Loew also controlled Loew's Theatrical Enterprises, which had over four hundred theaters nationwide. His son Arthur M. Loew—Arthur Jr.'s father—later became president of the theater group.

Unlike Chaplin, who had to take a job on occasion to supplement the stipend he received from his father, Loew was wealthy and didn't have to work at all. He took on creative assignments now and then, but he didn't really enjoy them. Arthur was a playboy and, at the time, seemed fiercely proud of it. But he was not merely a playboy. He had a quiet, intellectual side, one that delighted in long hours of conversation with a woman.

Joan had met Loew while she was still living with Chaplin. They saw each other socially on occasion, and though there was an immediate attraction she did not pursue it. "In my heart, I'm very monogamous," she once proclaimed. "I believe strongly in fidelity. I might be old-fashioned that way, but I think if you have a proper relationship with a man you don't want to go and ruin it. One of the most important things in life, other than health and a roof over your head, is loving somebody. And I'm very good at it." Yet, heartfelt as her declaration was, the candid Joan felt compelled to add, "I've been very good at it lots of times."

Loew was the first of Joan's inamoratos to take a real interest in her mental well-being. The first order of business, he felt, was to get her onto a psychiatrist's couch. At first, Joan resisted, feeling "there's an awful lot of rubbish attached to psychiatry." Loew didn't deny that, but urged her to go just the same. She laughingly agreed, and ended up staying in analysis on and off for the next four years—a relationship which outlasted the one she had with Loew. What Joan gained from her sessions was simple: "I learned," she reveals "to like myself [and] to respect my own opinions. Before that I had been a chameleon where men were concerned. If they wanted a clinging violet, I'd be that. If they wanted a football fan, I'd be that." Psychiatry, she says, taught her to be secure enough to tell a man, "Sorry, sweetie, but I don't want to."

As 1955 drew to a close, *The Virgin Queen* was scheduled to open in England. Joan was asked to go over for the October premiere, and Fox did not have to ask twice. "I haven't been home in eleven months," she told a reporter, and said she would be glad not only to see her family but to "just walk around," visiting her old haunts.

Joan felt doubly reborn, since she'd be arriving on Jackie's birthday and got to go on a buying spree before leaving Los Angeles. She bought records for her jazz-crazy sister, also buying her samples of the latest fashion crazes including plastic shoes, "the ones with glass heels. They look like glass slippers," she said. "She'll love them." Picking up "makeup gadgets," for her mother, slippers for her father and, in response to an urgent cable from Joe, "Davy Crockett things" for young Bill, she was off—arriving and being lambasted by her family, she says, for "sounding so American they could scarcely understand me."

Despite the communication gap it proved a delightful trip, made more so by her family's pride over her accomplishments. Even her father was thrilled, and Joan was at once surprised and touched to find that *he* was the keeper of the scrapbooks, ready to drag them out for visitors "at the drop of a hint," according to Elsa.

However, Elsa found Joan's stay more than a bit wearing. "A full house of Collinses is a thing to behold," she said, "providing you have the strength. Bill likes to retire to his room with the television set going full blast. Jackie prefers the radio in her room— usually turned up so that she can hear it if she suddenly decides to step into the kitchen. Add Joan, with her record player and being on the telephone, and you have something that closely resembles bedlam." Even when Joan was doing nothing, Elsa says, she was never at rest, "her fingers tapping the arm of the chair, her toes tapping the floor. She was constantly reaching for a cigarette, but her average was approximately two puffs per cigarette and then she put it out."

Withal, it was a delightful visit, and because of the closeness she felt for her family, leaving London for a second time was in some ways more difficult than it had been when Joan first went to Hollywood. If she had known what lay in wait just a few weeks down the road, she might well have stayed there and gone back to Rank.

As fate would have it, it wasn't long before Joan got the chance to put some of what she'd learned at analysis into practice. Maxwell Reed came bounding back into her life for the second time, only now he wasn't asking for money on the beach. He was asking for it in court.

While Joan was busy making her mark in Hollywood, Maxwell Reed had been more or less marking time.

At first, when she left him, Reed had refused to divorce his wife because he hoped for a reconciliation. When that clearly wasn't in the cards, he had stood by his decision for purely practical reasons. "I could never afford it," he said, meaning alimony. But then, as the months passed, a change came over Reed.

In July 1955, following literally in Joan's footsteps, he had attempted to realize his long-standing ambition of resettling in Hollywood, and flew over to make a decidedly second-rate syndicated TV series appropriately entitled *Captain David Grief*. While he was there, he did not contact Joan for help of any kind about roles in feature films. She probably would not have given it, but that was moot as far as he was concerned. His pride meant a lot to him just then, and his attitude was, "If I can't get a film on my own initiative, then I won't have it."

Unhappily, the series was short-lived and Reed couldn't get any other jobs. Brooding bitterly over his failure in Southern California, he returned to London a broken man. Certain that he would never work again, and convinced that Joan would never have become a Hollywood star had it not been for his encouragement, he decided that he was entitled to some of her earnings. The figure he arrived at was roughly $1,000 a month for support and, tacking on charges of cruelty and desertion, he went to court in March 1956 to get it.

Naturally, when Joan heard about the claim she was outraged by the sheer audacity of it. Responding in kind, she filed a cross-complaint the following month, asking for a divorce, and in May went before Judge Elmer Doyle in Santa Monica to recite a litany of Reed's evils. "He constantly made derogatory remarks about my appearance," she began, "and was consistently unfriendly to my friends and family, especially my sister. Generally he'd say I looked terrible. He said I had no talent as an actress and did not see how I would ever get a job. Once he met me at the airport and said I had aged ten years and later repeated that before our friends. He said I had better get all the work I could because by the time I was twenty-three I would be too old."

Young Jackie Collins flew in from England to corroborate her sister's testimony and, taken out of context, the evidence was indeed damning. Obviously, Joan never bothered to mention that a lot of what Reed said was made under circumstances of extreme stress, or was the kind of semi-innocent sarcasm in which both she and her husband frequently indulged.

Nonetheless, she had a strong case, and the result of the two claims was an uncontested divorce, which became final on July 8, 1957. Reed didn't get nearly what he wanted, but he came away with far more than Joan felt he deserved: the £500-odd in their British bank account, a cash award of £1,500, and £360 for his lawyer. In any event, that divorce case was virtually the last time Maxwell Reed would ever be in the public eye. *Helen of Troy*, released in 1955, was his last film, and in November of that year Maxwell Reed Enterprises went belly-up. Its creditors, principally the government and BOAC, claimed the company's assets (which amounted to a car and £115) to cover unpaid income taxes and a bounced check written a year before. Ironically, that check was the one Reed used to pay for his ill-fated trip to Hollywood.

Chapter Eight

＊＊＊＊＊＊＊＊＊＊＊＊＊＊＊＊＊＊＊＊＊＊＊＊＊＊＊＊＊

Although Joan was making a lot of money—she'd extended her pact to five years and had been raised to $1,750 a week—she never had very much of it in the bank. The divorce would prove expensive (her own legal fees amounted to nearly $4,000), but that was not entirely to blame.

The biggest drain was the extraordinary sums Joan was spending on clothes. The reason she gave was that her image as a serious actress was not well served by the flashy manner she'd adopted for Hollywood, continually stuffing herself into toreador pants, wearing shirts tied in the front, and poking her feet into thongs. One reporter happened to catch Joan at her most outrageous and described her taste: "Addicted to crazy hats, bizarre color schemes, gold fingernails and long dangling earrings, Joan also loves snug Jax matador pants in orange or shocking pink, which look as if they've been put on with a spray gun. The pants and a purple blouse constitute her favorite studio costume." The article went on to note: "Joan, who knows what she has and likes to display it, keeps the upper part of her blouse unbuttoned." Not to call too much attention to herself, she was fond of keeping her cigarettes and matches in her bra, where she had to go reaching whenever she wanted a smoke.

"I'm astonished that I could be such an idiot," she admitted to columnist Joe Hyams. "It's time I ceased to be identified as unwashed and uninhibited. I looked like a phony [and] if you don't mature as a person, how can you mature as an actress?" In her view, clothes were a way to achieve this end and, besides, she said, "I love clothes and I love getting dressed up."

Just how deep this love of hers ran is demonstrated by the fact that in the very same year she paid so much to be divorced from Reed, she went ahead and spent a whopping $20,000 on clothes. Discussing this with a reporter, she pointed to the mink she was wearing and said, "Arthur is very sweet. He gave me this stole. But I bought my own mink coat. And the beaver. And the other mink stole. The coat cost about six thousand dollars." Carting her wardrobe back to England for a visit amounted to a small fortune, setting her back $500 in excess baggage.

While Joan was busy switching lovers and changing her image offscreen, Fox lent her to MGM—coincidentally, Loew's studio—so that she could do some image-enhancing onscreen. The property was *The Opposite Sex*, a musical soap opera version of Clare Boothe Luce's *The Women*. Joan, of course, was standard-bearer for the bad girls; she played Crystal, a cold, husband-stealing vamp. Co-starring in this fine ensemble were June Allyson, Ann Miller, Carolyn Jones, and other MGM stars.

Unlike the trashy girls she played at Rank, Crystal was a trashy *woman*, one who hid her viperous nature beneath glamour and a silky-smooth manner. It was a larger-than-life part which Joan enjoyed—so much so that she would return to that kind of "bitch" character many times during her career. The only part of *The Opposite Sex* she *didn't* like was a scene which for over a decade stood as the most tedious and painful chore of her life.

During filming, Joan wrote the following curious note to her parents: "Dear Mummy and Daddy, Sorry for not writing sooner, and this is to say that all's well. Will get off a long letter within a couple of days, but right now I'm exhausted. Spent the dreariest day in the bathtub, wearing long underwear! Love, Joan."

For the next few days Elsa pondered the note, wondering if Hollywood had made her daughter quite mad. Finally, the promised letter arrived, putting the woman's mind at ease. She explained, "It seems that Joan had started the famed bathtub sequence for *The Opposite Sex* in a bathing suit, but the scene was a long one and took time to shoot. After three days in the tub, the suit was cutting her to ribbons and her skin was a combination of shades of black, blue and scarlet. The studio called in a doctor, who took one look at her and announced, 'No more water.' Consequently, on the fourth day Joan donned men's underwear, plus a pair of plastic trousers. They placed a wooden board in the tub, a plastic sheet around Joan's waist, then poured in water and soapflakes to give the bubble-bath effect on the top. In this way she was able to finish the scene, but she waited to write us the full details until she was able to *laugh* about them."

Like the bath, Joan's life looked great from the outside but was often painful to endure. Her career was on target and she was coming to enjoy the material side of stardom, not only the clothes but even lesser fascinations such as perfume, cars, and jewelry. "I'm twenty-three," she told one reporter. "I think it's about time I treated myself to diamonds." However, things still weren't jelling all around, especially where men were concerned.

Although she and Loew loved each other, when it came time for her to make a movie out of town early in 1956, she could not get him to promise he'd be faithful in her absence. She was ready to commit to him, even go so far as to consider marriage, but his male arrogance caused her skin to crawl. It reminded her of the days when her mother would connive to get a few dollars from her father, for she said at the time that she'd always "resented the freedom men have." Men, she said, could be forthright, whether asking a girl for a date or going after something in business, but let a woman try the same thing and she was labeled cheap and scheming. That didn't suit Joan at all for, she says, "I hate playing games."

Fortunately, although Loew's attitude annoyed her, she didn't have to deal with it just then. She'd been set to do the sunken treasure film *Boy on a Dolphin* with Alan Ladd, but that part went to an actress making her American film debut, one who Fox also thought had potential—Sophia Loren. Instead, in the oddest casting stroke to hit Hollywood in years, Joan was given the lead in *Sea Wife*. Based on the novel by J. M. Scott, it's the story of four people who, after their boat is torpedoed in the Second World War, are stranded on an island. What was unusual about having Joan as one of the castaways, is that the former bad girl of Britain, and more recently the man-eating star of *The Girl In the Red Velvet Swing* and the husband-stealing siren of *The Opposite Sex*, would be playing a nun.

Joan got the part not because Fox was keen on broadening her as an actress, but because the picture's director wanted her. Brilliant and mercurial, Italian filmmaker Roberto Rossellini was best known not by what he did on film, but what he did off camera. In 1950 he left his wife to live with actress Ingrid Bergman (who also left her husband) and whom he would leave in 1957 to carry on with Indian screenwriter Somali Das Gupta. Rossellini was to make his American screen debut with *Sea Wife* and, after seeing Joan as Evelyn Nesbit, felt she had both the innocent and sexual qualities the part required.

"I was just as surprised as anyone when Rossellini picked me for the part," she said, adding that she was not only flattered and excited but more than a little anxious; this was the perfect opportunity to show the world that she was more than just "torrid baggage," as the *New York Times* had snidely dismissed her. "This sex business gets to me," she said at the time, taking particular exception to people who accused her of trying to imitate Monroe. "They talk about my stance and walk. It's true that I do walk with a sort of wiggle-waggle. I was kidded about it back in school in England, and I made a definite effort to correct it. But it's hard to change a lifetime habit." She hoped that rather than have to get rid of what she called her "oomph," she could use the film to emphasize her other qualities. "I'm ready to meet the challenge," she said, "to prove myself as an actress."

Sea Wife was scheduled to be shot on location in Jamaica and in London, the latter being where Rossellini was headquartered for preproduction—casting, polishing the script, and conferring with the creative team on the film. The week after she appeared in divorce court, Joan flew to London to meet the fifty-year-old director and to begin preparing for the role. Before leaving, she turned her apartment over to Jackie, who had recently been tossed out of school. Her teenage sister had the place virtually to herself for nearly a year, during which time she says she contacted everyone in Joan's address book. The result, Jackie revealed years after becoming a successful novelist, was that "in that time [I] learnt everything that I have been writing about ever since. I owed it all to her." Years later, Jackie would repay the favor and get her own career going when she wrote what would prove to be the most important film role of her sister's career.

Joan's preparations in London included the usual duties, such as arriving at a suitably shapeless wardrobe and coming up with makeup that wouldn't look as though she was wearing makeup. However, she would also be doing research as well—more, as it happens, than she'd ever done for a part. The reasons were practical as well as creative. "Because I am not Catholic," she says, "I wanted to be sure I didn't commit any offense."

With her hair cut short so she would "feel" like a nun, Joan spent time at a convent "meeting and talking to a lot of nuns, who have been very helpful. Not cold and remote, as I thought they might be." She also read every book she could find about Catholicism, went to church regularly, and talked to friends who were Catholic. After several intensive weeks she went to Jamaica, where Rossellini had gone to scout for suitable locations. As it turned out, that was all he'd ever do on the film.

Personally and artistically, Rossellini was not known for his restraint. Already frayed at the edges because he'd had to fly to Jamaica (Ingrid Bergman said of his fear, "Years before, he'd had this overwhelming premonition that if he ever flew, harm would come to Robertino [their son],") he was startled to learn that Fox was unwilling to let him shoot the film as he wished. His idea was to have Joan and a fellow castaway, an RAF pilot played by Richard Burton, become sexually involved. Fox, fearing a backlash from the Catholic community, didn't even want them to share a kiss. He was insistent but so was the studio, and with the cast and crew inactive to the tune of thousands of dollars a day, Fox told production manager Bob McNaught to start directing the film. Rossellini waited a few days to see if the studio would come around; when it seemed content to leave McNaught in the driver's seat, he angrily thumbed his nose at the project and returned to London. His departure left *Sea Wife* in the hands of a well-meaning man who was highly qualified to oversee the logistical aspects of a film, from transportation to scheduling to budget, but hadn't the remotest idea how to motivate an actor—certainly not as Rossellini would have done.

Joan was crushed, not merely because of the artistic void she felt under McNaught's direction, but because she had talked the picture up to the London press, making a point of telling them that they wouldn't have Joan Collins to kick around anymore. She was about to show them she could act. All she ended up showing anyone was that she looked great with a minimum of makeup. Also annoying was that even if she had wanted to mount a protest, refuse to make the picture, her co-star was not going to support her. Fox had made Richard Burton into a star with *The Robe* in 1953, but he followed that hit with a string of flops and had just endured some unusually harsh criticism during a season at the Old Vic in London. In a dour frame of mind, and doing the film solely to fulfill his contractual obligations to the studio, he was equally blasé about Rossellini and McNaught. Thus, what could have been an exotic

and challenging film emerged as an insipid, para-
noiacally tame soap opera.

If Burton was creatively numb, other parts of him
were very much alive. Years later, after losing the part
of Cleopatra to Elizabeth Taylor, Joan said, "If I'd
made it, I wouldn't have married Burton, that's for
sure. I'd worked with him once before, and that was
quite enough for me."

Though Burton was a serious actor, he also had the
reputation of being an equally serious womanizer.
Raymond Massey, his co-star in a different film, was
once asked by another actor if there were any woman
Burton had *not* managed to seduce.

"Yes," said Massey, after thinking hard for a
moment. "Marie Dressler."

"But she's dead!" rejoined the other.

"Yes, I know," was Massey's reply.

Though Burton was married to Sybil at the time, he
very much wanted to add Joan to his list of conquests. She, however, was not interested in him—at
least not that way, as a notch on his gun. "He always
said I was the only leading lady he never got into his
bed," she says. "He felt I shouldn't break his record,
but that was one I was *happy* to break." For the two
months they were in Jamaica she was constantly
parrying his advances and allusions. The inconvenience factor was minimal, for Joan was accustomed to
wolves; what seems to have bothered her more than
his disappointing and often tiresome company were
his "Rabelaisian habits . . . staying out until the
early hours" and coming to the set with red eyes and
liquor on his breath. Like Bogart, Gable, and so many
others she'd admired from afar, Richard Burton had
feet of clay; no wonder she had no desire to find out
what the rest of him was like.

While Burton could be sent scurrying with a few
cutting words or a deprecating laugh, once during
her stay Joan went up against a somewhat slimier
predator. It was between takes, and Joan—the "ex-

pert swimmer"—was loosening up with a few strokes at sea when she spotted two large green spheres shimmering several yards away. Paddling over, she was unable to make the objects out and called to some crew members swimming nearby. They came, they saw, and they promptly left, dragging the confused actress between them. Upon reaching the shore, Joan's colleagues shivered reflexively and informed her that the green spheres were eyes and that she had been moments away from angering a very large octopus. Joan took the news in stride, although nowadays her preferred form of exercise is sit-ups.

Chapter Nine

•••

After eight weeks on location, Joan went back to London to finish *Sea Wife*, which she was not in the least bit enthusiastic about doing. Rossellini's departure stripped away Joan's passion for the film; now it was just a job. Interiors and scenes in a huge water tank were filmed at Elstree Studios in Borehamwood so Joan lived at Harley House and commuted each morning.

Returning to Los Angeles, Joan quickly got back into the swing of her life. She learned that she'd have less than a month before being shuttled off to another film, *Island in the Sun*, which was being shot on yet another location. Thus, she used her free month primarily to unwind which, for Joan, meant a lot of dancing—her great catharsis. Even when she was working, there was always a cha-cha record playing in her one-room apartment. She'd turn on calypso or

Afro-Cuban music before she got out of bed in the morning—at six-thirty during a film, eleven when she was idle—dance while she got ready for the day, and keep it on for as long as she was in the house. Even when she was with people, she liked to have the music going, as a kind of ambient sponge which she could use to soak up some of the energy that was constantly building inside of her. When she went out, nothing made her happier than to go to clubs which, if they weren't as exceptional as those in London, had the kind of music that let her keep on "jiving all night."

Despite this hyperactivity, Joan had become very disciplined since joining Fox. The music was a release, and one she dearly loved, but work was still foremost in her mind. She would not stay out past ten or eleven o'clock when she was shooting and, much as she detested getting up early in the morning, was never late. Back in London, her mother had been pleased to note, "Although Joan is on the run from the moment she gets up in the morning until she climbs into bed at night, I'm delighted that she has learned to channel her energy." She'd had to, of course, since the demands on her time were such that disorder would have ended her career.

At the same time, her confidence was at an all-time high. She was constantly being filmed, photographed, quoted, and feted as a great new "find." In fact, more than one columnist referred to Joan, Rita Moreno, and Natalie Wood as the actresses who would turn out to be that decade's answer to Ava Gardner, Rita Hayworth, and Lana Turner. This built her ego and reinforced what she was learning in analysis, that there really wasn't a need for her to try to be all things to all people—a boy to get her father's attention, a Slob to fit in at RADA, a slave to satisfy a husband or lover. It was okay to loosen up, to be whatever she wanted to be, to *like* herself. Pampering herself with clothes and jewelry were the bellwethers of this new independence; so was her uncharacteristic handling of the relationship with Arthur Loew.

Loew had visited briefly in Jamaica, which made for a pleasant interlude. Joan, however, felt the rendezvous had been romantically superficial. His inability to devote himself to her, compounded by the length of time they had been apart during the first half of 1956, froze the relationship at the level of friendship rather than ardor. Instead of fighting to change that, or smiling sweetly and tolerating the double standard of his infidelity and her faithfulness (as she might have done mere months before), Joan just let the relationship stay where it was while she went away and made her movies. At the same time, she dated not only Loew but Michael Rennie, Robert Wagner, conductor Buddy Bregman and, incredibly, Sydney Chaplin's older brother Charles Jr.—among others. She wasn't as happy as she'd have been in a good one-to-one relationship but, as compromises went, this wasn't a bad one.

Island in the Sun was based on a novel published in 1956 by Alec Waugh, brother of Evelyn. Set in the West Indies, the film consists of several interwoven stories. The cast included James Mason, Joan Fontaine, Michael Rennie, Harry Belafonte, and Joan.

Darryl Zanuck had read the novel and bought it at once for the screen, fascinated by its daring interracial relationships, which is ironic, given what he'd done to emasculate *Sea Wife*. Ultimately, however, Zanuck's good intentions proved to be a front. Joan Fontaine says that Zanuck knew early on that "it was too soon to tackle the race question with honesty" and, despite the very vocal protests of Waugh, he never really intended to try. What he was interested in was the publicity the film would generate just by being made. And the backlash was indeed enormous, both during and after production. Fontaine said that she received "hundreds of reviling letters [which] read 'If you're so hard up that you have to work with a nigger . . .'" and South Carolina went so far as to introduce legislation that would have fined theaters $5,000 for showing the film. Of course, no one had seen it at the time and *Island in the Sun* proved to be a tempest in a teapot, being essentially a CinemaScope travelogue with handsome actors doing little more than flirting. But the controversy generated public interest, which outweighed the bad reviews and made for good box-office results—just as Zanuck had planned.

Whatever the studio's motives, Joan had a great time making the film. Not that she liked the script ("Not very good, was it?") or the director, Robert Rossen ("The cast was left pretty much on our own— he usually printed the second take") or the fact that she had to fight for the relatively juicy role of Jocelyn (Zanuck had originally wanted her to do the part played by Patricia Owens). What she liked was spending the late summer of 1956 on location in Barbados and Grenada. The days were short because they'd start to lose the light late in the afternoon, so there was a lot of time for rest, relaxation—and romance. But if Joan had flouted convention by living with Sydney Chaplin, this time she was in a situation which made even *her* nervous.

Harry Belafonte was one of the most popular entertainers in the world. The twenty-nine-year-old singer from New York's Harlem had started his career as an actor with the American Negro Theater, before becoming a nightclub singer and, in time, the King of Calypso. Movies were natural for him, and *Island in the Sun* was his third, following *Bright Ròad* and *Carmen Jones*.

Having ended his first marriage right before filming began, Belafonte was not only eligible but extremely desirable. He was at the height of his fame and Joan found him cool and charming, possessing a quiet sexuality in his electric gaze, easy movements, and voice—which was as smooth in conversation as it was onstage. It also didn't hurt that he sang calypso, one of Joan's favorite kinds of music.

Fresh from the unromantic Loew and scorekeeping Burton, Joan was ripe for someone to sweep her off her feet. With his commanding sensuality, gracious manners, and class, Belafonte was the man to do it; and the balmy, sun-drenched West Indies was definitely the *place* to do it. But, at first, Joan was extremely self-conscious about even being seen alone with him, largely because many of the crew members were friends and she didn't want them either trying to protect her virtue from the "ravenous black man" or, conversely, thinking that what the newspapers said about her was true, that she was nothing more than a hot little number and an easy mark. She also didn't want to compound the controversy surrounding the film by sleeping with a black man and risking a scandal, although Harry would himself marry Julie Robinson, a white woman, in April 1957. Oddly enough, the question of conscience didn't seem to bother Joan, since she had never tried to delude herself into believing that Loew was being faithful to her.

Yet when all was said and done, Joan wanted Belafonte, he wanted her, and when they were back in Los Angeles, away from the West Indies fishbowl, they ended up as lovers. They were both at the same Hollywood party when Harry came over and asked for her address. Joan told him and left the party shortly thereafter. At home she traded the cocktail dress she'd been wearing for a less restrictive caftan, poured herself a brandy, and answered the doorbell. There stood Harry, wearing pants that fit him like a second skin and with his shirt provocatively open; the air fairly crackled with desire, and it did not take long for them to put the weeks of anticipation behind them.

They continued to meet—discreetly, lest the press get wind of it—but it was to be a very brief affair.

Harry was also seeing his longtime friend Julie, and when they learned in November that she was pregnant the singer decided to marry her. However, his brief time with Joan would remain one of the few liaisons which she'd remember with only fond, loving thoughts.

Joan continued to see Arthur Loew, but they were mostly casual get-togethers—dinner dates, movies, and the like—and even that came to an end in December. Now playing the field, she actually dated fourteen different men in a two-week period, one man each night. Interestingly enough, what she found after a few months of this was that "there really are very few attractive men in Hollywood. I like a man with a sense of humor, and most young men take themselves so seriously. I like a man who is masculine, and," she said ruefully, "so few men really are."

Joan certainly didn't take it all that seriously, being content, she says, "to table-hop through life." However, she learned so much by flitting from man to man that she actually agreed to do a one-shot contribution to a major women's magazine, confidently dispensing dating advice. Among her thoughts:

How to Lead Him On
Make your own special kind of sex appeal come alive with plenty of humor. Don't try serious marriage talk; let him *think* you couldn't care less about tying him down.
How to Draw the Line
When he gets that certain gleam in his eye, a carefully timed joke will kid him out of it. To lose a wolf, start talking marriage.
What Mother Might Not Tell You
Be a "man's woman" if you want to win a certain guy; avoid "girl talk" on your double dates and

keep away from hen sessions at parties. To lose a
wolf, use opposite tactics—they work!

But the social whirl was more than just man-
stalking. Joan did it to help keep her mind off the
mounting disappointment she was feeling with Fox.
Though neither *Sea Wife* nor *Island in the Sun* had been
released, she was distressed with their creative failure and found herself doing something that was
politically unwise, criticizing the studio by telling the
press that she wished Hollywood would spend as
much time on scripts as it did on "the style of one's
eyelashes."

Not that Joan didn't campaign hard for quality
roles. She did. For example, when she read the script
for a new movie being readied at Fox, *Oh Men! Oh
Women!*, she "begged and pleaded" for the part. It
was a comedy, and the kind of thing she'd been dying
to do. But Barbara Rush got the film; perhaps
coincidentally, Joan had recently spurned the sexual
advances of Darryl Zanuck, which may have had
some impact on the casting. Joan also lobbied for a
film version of the play she had done, *The Skin of Our
Teeth*, but while plays were bought for other stars,
Zanuck nixed that purchase as well. The cigar-
chomping mogul had other plans for Joan.

Since he had reaped a good deal of publicity by
making Joan a nun and then giving her "colored
blood," Zanuck decided to make her a real tramp this
time around by co-starring her in *The Wayward Bus*.
The picture was based on John Steinbeck's 1947 novel
about a group of people stranded overnight at a way
station in California. Jayne Mansfield starred as a
cheap dancer yearning for the big time, Dan Dailey
was an alcoholic salesman, and Joan was the cheap,
heavy-drinking manager of the diner who has a
heated fling with Rick Jason.

Her hair and makeup a mess, her clothes baggy
and unflattering, Joan was a revelation to those who

thought she couldn't act. Unfortunately when the picture was released in 1957 it was such an artistic and commercial disaster that not even Joan's being cast against type got much notice. The consensus among critics was that director Victor Vicas had reduced Steinbeck's textured characters to stereotypes spouting flat, hackneyed dialogue. Joan *did* receive fine notices, but the film was such a flop it failed to do what she had hoped—break her out of the pack of would-be superstars on the Fox lot.

Joan took the setback pragmatically. She said that she'd learned from the beleaguered Vicas more about acting and opening up than from anyone she'd ever worked with, and she also came away with a healthy regard for her own professionalism. It came about in a strange way. One day on the lot, Joan reports, she went to co-star Mansfield's motor home to review a scene. Entering, she discovered the buxom blonde "standing there, one leg up on a chair," while "the makeup people shaved her crotch." Joan had to wait until they were done, which reassured her that even if she wasn't getting all the breaks, at least her priorities were in order.

The year 1956 had been an unexpectedly disapointing one for Joan. She'd lost a husband, found and lost two lovers, and made three bad films back to back. She was even suspended briefly for refusing to do a Richard Widmark western called *The Last Wagon*, which she felt was a picture that gave her nothing more to do than say to the hero, "I saw a man go *that* way." However, Joan didn't make a practice of turning down parts—not yet, anyway—because she needed her weekly paycheck.

During this period, her family provided the only real comfort to her. She encouraged Jackie, whom she describes as "ravishingly beautiful and very clever," to accept an offer from Ealing to do a small part opposite Alec Guinness in the British film *Barnacle Bill*

(U.S. title: *All at Sea*), the story of a sailor who turns a dilapidated pier into a landlocked pleasure cruiser for the seasick. Jackie was fourteenth-billed as "June" but, unimpressed with the experience, decided to stick to writing. Joan fully understood, and was quick to support her in that decision as well. In addition to Jackie, their father had come over for a visit late in the year, and Joan found it comforting to have him around to pick her up at the studio at the end of each day.

But what she *really* wanted was a hit and, short of sleeping with her boss, she was going to do everything she could to have one.

Chapter Ten

◆◆◆◆◆◆◆◆◆◆◆◆◆◆◆◆◆◆◆◆◆◆◆◆◆◆◆◆◆◆◆◆◆◆◆

*A*fter *The Wayward Bus* was in the can, Joan vacationed in Acapulco. Since there was no film in the offing and she was collecting her $2,000 a week anyway, she stayed for the entire month of January, content to do absolutely nothing but soak up "all that sunshine, the exclusive company, the private beaches, and the lovely banditos" (a favorite drink of hers, consisting of bananas, apricots, rum, and cream).

When she got back, Joan curtailed some of her flitting about, spending time with friends like Sammy Davis, Jr., agent Billy Belasco, Fox contract player Joanne Woodward and her companion Paul Newman, James Mason and his wife, and seeing a lot of the inordinately wealthy twenty-nine-year-old Nicky Hilton. The son of Hilton Hotel czar Conrad Hilton,

Nicky boasted to women that between himself, his father, and his brother they possessed "a yard of cock," and he was not averse to flagging *his* share around. Although he had impetuously married Elizabeth Taylor not quite seven years before, they were divorced after seven months and Nicky went back to sowing his wild oats—Natalie Wood and Joan among them. But Joan had had enough of chronic playboys and Nicky, with his affinity for gambling and drugs, was one of her less enduring relationships. She would continue seeing him on and off for over a year, after which they went their separate ways. Not long thereafter, Nicky's fondness for drugs cost him his life.

Joan's next picture was one she was unusually loath to do. Not only was the script truly horrible, but she was being sent to yet another location, this one not nearly as refreshing as the last two. But Joan, along with Robert Wagner, had no choice but to obey their masters at Fox, so early in 1957 they were en route to Japan for *Stopover Tokyo.*

What the filmmakers did, remarkably enough, was to take John P. Marquand's Mr. Moto novel of the same name, do away with the Oriental sleuth, and replace him with Robert Wagner as an American counterintelligence agent trying to prevent the Soviets from blowing up the American high commissioner during a public appearance. Joan was assigned the role of Tina, Wagner's lover, a part that *Variety* would later call nothing more than "a lovely scenic addition."

Joan found both the picture and Japan a bore. Wagner was off limits, since he had just made Natalie Wood his fiancée, and the crew members were busy exploring the exotic Japanese night life, enjoying the women and saki equally. That left Joan to her own devices which, after seeing the sights and shopping for clothes, meant spending most of her time in her hotel room.

Returning to Hollywood, Joan was really beginning to tire of the window-dressing parts she was doing, and told one reporter, "I'm afraid I'll be a has-been before I'm finished being promising." Yet it's likely she'd rather have done a few more of those than what Fox had planned for her—which was nothing. Darryl Zanuck had abruptly left the studio in 1956, setting up an independent production company and turning Fox over to Spyros Skouras. The forceful Greek had his hands full with problems, ranging from Marilyn Monroe's temperament to a lot of red ink at the studio; he did not, however, have his hands full of Joan, which was something he wanted in a more literal sense. Whether that was the reason Joan didn't work, or whether if was simply Skouras's absorption with more important matters, or the fact that every picture she made flopped—most likely a combination of the three—Joan's inactivity continued through 1957, broken only by the time she spent traveling to promote her films.

The first break in the monotony came in June, when she plugged *The Wayward Bus*, flying from New York to Antibes, in the South of France, for a vacation with her mother and sister. But most of her time was spent lunching with girlfriends, shopping, and listening to records. She even tried to start a fashion trend. Tired of plunging necklines and looking for something with "more subtle" sex appeal, she created sackcloth dresses which drooped and sagged and allowed a lot more freedom of movement. What's more, she found herself daydreaming wistfully about what would happen if she gave up acting to become a clothes designer, which was a close second in her heart.

There were still no serious romantic involvements in her life but that, at least, was about to change dramatically.

In November 1957, Joan went to New York to promote *Stopover Tokyo*, doing countless press inter-

views, attending a concert by Pat Boone at the Roxy
just to be photographed and seen, and appearing
with Robert Wagner on TV programs like *The Ed
Sullivan Show*, where she unintentionally embarrassed her co-star on the air by saying of his impending
marriage, "Good luck—you'll need it." Though she
admits the comment was inappropriate in any case,
what she'd *meant* to do was caution him about the
institution of marriage itself, and not the spunky
Natalie Wood.

Before flying to New York, Joan arranged to have
dinner there with George Englund. The thirty-one-
year-old writer/director had married actress Cloris
Leachman in 1953, and the couple had been frequent
companions of Joan and both Sydney Chaplin and
Arthur Loew. He was going east on business, and
would help Joan keep her spirits up for a chore she
did not relish—talking about a picture she hadn't
liked when she read the script, and liked even less
now that she'd seen the finished product.

Englund was the kind of man Joan might well have
designed as the ideal all-around male. Standing six
foot two, with arresting green eyes and a manner as
elegant as his dress, he had a sense of humor more
refined than Chaplin, a style more gracious than
Loew, and native intelligence greater than that of any
of Joan's other lovers. He was also one of the most
giving men Joan had ever met.

When the two met for dinner at the Little Club in
Manhattan it was innocent enough, just a continua-
tion of the kind of get-together they had all the time
in Los Angeles. But there was one major difference:
they were alone in New York. Joan had had her fill of
sitting across the table from Hollywood types who
were shallow or supercilious or interested only in
getting her into bed. Here was someone who enjoyed
her for her company and for her conversation—and
who was everything she admired in a man besides.

Against every instinct she found herself getting
funny inside, not only enjoying him but *wanting* him;

by the time they had walked back to his hotel room, she didn't know which was the stronger emotion— her desire or her guilt. This was the husband of a friend. Although it was a friend whom, Englund assured her, he would eventually divorce because she was extremely difficult to live with (an editor for *People* would later dub Leachman one of Hollywood's "certifiable crazies"), Joan did not want ot help him cheat on her.

Nonetheless, Joan's heart and libido ganged up on her ethics and, paving the road to hell with her good intentions, she ended up sleeping with Englund. For his part, Englund has never said what his own feelings were upon finding himself attracted to Joan. But whether she was just an amusement for New York who got out of hand, or whether her beauty, grace, and attentiveness were qualities he desperately needed, it is doubtful that he would have started with her had he foreseen the emotional entanglements which would dog them both for a period of nearly two long years.

During the few days they were together in New York, Joan experienced ecstasy when they were together, suffering when they were apart, and burning dread and confusion whenever she thought about what would happen when they left their love nest and returned to Los Angeles. For as much as they unburdened themselves to each other in New York, Englund never told Joan when he would leave his wife, or managed to convince her that he could endure being apart from his three young children.

At the time, Joan was living in an apartment on Shoreham Drive, a short, flat road which lies just above Sunset Boulevard, and she was to grow far more familiar with that apartment than she would have liked. The telephone was her lifeline to Englund and, like a teenager, she waited for it to ring. When he'd call, it was invariably a quick hello stolen while Leachman was out or when a meeting had broken up;

instructions on where to meet; or—the one she came
to dread—word that he would be unable to keep a
planned rendezvous. Joan had never had to deal with
being stood up, not just because it rarely happened,
but because if it did she was resilient enough to put
the man out of her mind and go out dancing.
However, there was no getting George Englund off
her mind.

For the most part, she didn't have to. Since Joan
was not working through the end of 1957 and early
1958, and Englund's own schedule was usually flex-
ible, they managed to get together at least every other
day. Sometimes they would go to a restaurant far
from town and do nothing but enjoy being together;
other times they would go to Joan's apartment. And
then there were those times that they would get
together and fight.

Like a torn thread in a large piece of fabric, the
problem they had was a small one at first. Though
Joan dutifully waited for Englund to give her a yea or
nay about when and where to meet, when he
couldn't see her she refused to stay home. Part of that
was sheer frustration over whatever circumstances
had kept them apart; part of it was her innate
impatience. Joan was antsy enough collecting her
salary for doing absolutely nothing; she wasn't about
to sit around and dwell on how much she was
missing Englund. Even the efforts of an astrologer
friend—Joan was coming to rely more and more on
the stars—and her analyst were not enough to help
her keep the catch-as-catch-can nature of the relationship in perspective.

Englund, alas, was not terribly understanding
about Joan's need to get out, especially when she
went with another man, as she often did. Although
these dates were platonic, Englund did not take to
them kindly. He couldn't understand why Joan was
unwilling to inconvenience herself while he sorted
out his personal matters; for her part, Joan couldn't

understand why he was getting upset over what she assured him were nonsexual, nonemotional nights out with the likes of Nicky Hilton. (He failed to grasp the fact that Joan actually *preferred* platonic dates, saying that it prevented "fights in the taxi on the way home" which she found just "too exhausting!")

On one level, of course, Englund was simply jealous of his beautiful, lusty lover. She made no bones about enjoying sex, and there was catch-22: If he was willing to cheat on his wife, what was to stop Joan doing the same to him, the old what's-good-for-the-goose-is-good-for-the-gander syndrome? On a different level entirely, it's likely that Englund wanted to make sure Joan would be there when he finally left Leachman. He was having a much more difficult time effecting the break than he'd anticipated, making several false starts by removing himself in stages from his wife's bed, and then from the house—only to return. The thought of Joan seeing other men had to be anything but reassuring.

In the early weeks of 1958, Joan finally got herself a picture. It was, again, not the kind of film she'd have chosen for herself: an action-filled western. Not being physically inclined, Joan had never even ridden a horse. Worse, she had only a few days to learn how before being shipped to the movie's Mexican locations.

But it was work, and she was going to be co-starring with one of the most popular actors in the world, so Joan undertook *The Bravados*. Gregory Peck starred in the uncustomary role of a vigilante with Joan on hand simply to pretty up the screen, this time as Peck's lover.

After training at the ranch maintained by Fox for what she complains was a mere "nine hours on a well-trained pony," Joan flew to Mexico City and was driven several hours northwest to the city of Morelia. There, she and her colleagues were put up at a crumbling motel "far from any nearby town [for] six long, dreary weeks." Her record player was her best friend during the month and a half, especially on the days when she had to ride. She claims that director Henry King "put me on the wildest horses in Mexico; I was never so terrified," and adds that while "there were always expert cowboys close at hand," she never had a more difficult acting job than trying to play "the world's greatest rider [because] I was absolutely frozen when a horse came near me."

Though she acknowledges that there were occasional displays of temper because they were all "cooped up on location," for the most part she, Peck, and King got along very well. Joan was especially grateful to Peck who, though a expert horseman, usually restrained his own mount instead of forcing her to keep up with him.

Still, it was a rough experience for Joan and, upon returning to Los Angeles to film the interiors, she confided to Louella Parsons in all sincerity, "That I am alive . . . is a miracle." Nonetheless, she was glad she'd done the picture. "It's a marvelous western," she told columnist Sheilah Graham, "but I genuinely feel that a girl is out of place in a western. She's only put in for the sake of sexy ads. But it was wonderful to work with Gregory Peck. It's the only way to make stars in this business—for a girl to be put opposite a big star."

Regardless of the truth of what she said, Joan was getting tired of being tacked on to movies. She didn't know how, but she decided that if Fox didn't come up with more suitable properties very soon, she would take matters into her own hands.

Chapter Eleven

◆◆◆◆◆◆◆◆◆◆◆◆◆◆◆◆◆◆◆◆◆◆◆◆◆◆◆◆◆◆◆◆◆◆

As it turned out, Englund's fears about Joan's infidelity turned out to be something of a self-fulfilling prophecy.

After returning from Mexico, Joan was right back into the on-again, off-again marriage of Englund and Leachman, and she began to believe that he would *never* leave his wife, especially now that they'd learned Cloris was going to have another baby. Joan was irked that he'd let that happen, though Englund insisted that the pregnancy was the result of just one night together, when he'd had to assure her that the rumors of an affair with Joan Collins weren't true (his car had been spotted outside her apartment).

Joan didn't understand why, instead of hopping into bed with her, he hadn't seized that opportunity to make the break, and they argued violently. Joan was hurt and disappointed. For a man who usually spoke and acted with great conviction, Englund was taking an awfully long time to come to terms with what he had convinced her was inevitable. Joan could relate to his fears and didn't want to pressure him with demands of her own, but she was beginning to doubt that the divorce was ever going to happen, and that made her bitter.

Tired of being the dutiful "other woman," Joan poured her heart out to friend Zsa Zsa Gabor one afternoon. She'd decided to go to New York to get away from Englund and the confusion of their

romantic triangle, and Gabor talked her into taking a
little side trip to see a friend of hers, Rafael Trujillo,
who had told her he would love to meet Joan. The
twenty-nine-year-old son of the President (read: dic-
tator) of the Dominican Republic, Trujillo was described by Zsa Zsa as exceedingly handsome, very
bright, exquisitely mannered, and as wealthy as they
come. Trujillo had parked his yacht in Palm Beach,
where he had gone on business, and Zsa Zsa
arranged to have Trujillo's private plane meet Joan in
New York and whisk her to Florida.

In a strictly physical sense, if Joan ever had a type
of man to whom she was most attracted, it was the
Latin lover. And Trujillo was that, fully living up to
Zsa Zsa'a description of him. After throwing an
elegant party on the boat, with political and rich
figures in attendance, Trujillo persuaded Joan to stay
the night on his yacht. Ordinarily, she would have
refused out of consideration to Englund. But she was
tipsy, she'd been won over by her utterly gracious
and accommodating host, and she was still extremely
angry with Englund for having made his wife pregnant. The last time she'd been hurt by a man, Arthur
Loew, she'd thanked him by sleeping with Harry
Belafonte; this time it was Englund on the receiving
end, his loss being Trujillo's gain.

Joan's trip east lasted only a week since, in a fit of
magnanimity, Fox had given her another picture to
do. But before she left, she received a gift from
Trujillo, a necklace worth some $10,000. Though she
felt awkward accepting such a costly present, she was
thrilled to add the piece to her little collection.

The movie at Fox was *Rally 'Round the Flag, Boys!*
and Joan was excited to be doing it. This was the kind
of film she'd been dying to make—a comedy. However, she was given the picture not because the studio
had become enlightened or forgiving, but because of

the intensive lobbying by the stars, Joan's friends Paul Newman and Joanne Woodward. They knew that Joan would be an asset to the film, and convinced the studio that if nothing else she was a far better actress than Jayne Mansfield, whom the filmmakers wanted to co-star. Though the studio had been anxious to collect a hefty fee by loaning Joan out to United Artists for the Burt Lancaster/Kirk Douglas film *The Devil's Disciple*, they capitulated.

Rally 'Round the Flag, Boys! was based on a novel by Max Shulman, the story of a small town called Putnam's Landing, whose residents resist the military's plan to build a missile base in their midst. Joan had the time of her life on the film as what she calls "a witchy vamp [who] spends the major part of the picture plotting to get Paul Newman from his wife, played by Joanne." About *Stopover Tokyo* and *The Bravados* she had said, "I was terrible in those and didn't belong in them," but in *Rally 'Round the Flag, Boys!* she was in her element. "I play a character as nearly myself as possible, except this is a caricature," she said. "Actually, this girl is what I would like to be: terribly uninhibited. She has a tremendous zest for life and a great sense of humor about herself. She is completely irrepressible. Nothing but nothing fazes her; she's a gay, fun-loving person."

Not only did Joan love the character, but she especially loved Woodward and Newman, describing the latter as "a smashing person, and a joy to work with in every way—funny, warm, caring, absolutely the antithesis of a movie star." The three of them laughed a lot and clowned around on the set, leaving Joan feeling wonderful and pleased that "at long last I've done a good job in a movie, [playing] a real three-dimensional character." In August, just after completing the film, she said to Joe Hyams, "You wait and see. I'll be extremely good in this picture."

Joan was right, the critics all agreeing that she was marvelous. Sadly, it did her little good since the rest of the actors and the film itself were universally trashed. And with good reason: the subtle, pointed wit of the book had been turned into broad, clumsy comedy on the screen. Newman was singularly unconvincing, hamming unmercifully and making a fool of himself. To no one's surprise, the picture was a commercial disaster, giving Joan her fifth box-office flop in a row. Fox couldn't help but wonder if they might have done better with Jayne Mansfield and, without a Paul Newman to champion her, Joan didn't work again for nearly a year.

Meanwhile, things weren't much better on the domestic front. The George Englund roller coaster continued to take her for a ride, only now the peaks and valleys were becoming much steeper than before.

Joan and Englund had made up when she came back from New York, at which time the latter grimly informed Joan that his wife had had a miscarriage. He evidently blamed himself to some degree, since they'd been having vicious fights before she lost the child; it was at times like this that Joan still felt stirrings of conscience, for Englund should have been home comforting his wife instead of going out and dining with his lover. However, as guilty as she may have felt, Joan wasn't above calling Leachman shortly after the miscarriage and boldly bringing up her involvement with George. Leachman says that Joan phoned one morning informing her, "George just left here . . . I'm in love with your husband," after which Joan allegedly demanded, "What are you going to do about it?" Leachman didn't know quite what to say, and asked glibly, "Well, do you think you two can make a go of it?" Joan answered without hesitation, "Yes, I do," then added with a keen edge of frustration, "But he loves you!"

Although Joan obviously realized this, Englund apparently did not. He assured Joan that at long last the marriage was finally over; he'd even started divorce proceedngs and wanted to marry Joan.

Suddenly, Leachman and Trujillo and moviemaking were all pushed to the back of her mind. In typical Joan Collins fashion, she gave the world what her lover was giving her. When she and Sydney Chaplin had fallen in love in Italy, his smugness and sarcasm became her modus operandi on the set of *Land of the Pharaohs*; now, in the midst of making *Rally 'Round the Flag, Boys!*, the joy of acting in that picture became even greater as she radiated love and contentment. But that satisfaction was short-lived. During the shoot, the couple attended a fancy Hollywood party at the ultrachic Romanoff's, and Joan foolishly wore the Trujillo necklace. Why not? she reasoned. Only a few close friends knew how she had gotten it, and they were discreet—except, as it happened, when they were tipsy. When one of those close girlfriends ambled over and asked Joan point-blank if her necklace was the one Trujillo had given her, Englund saw red. A flustered Joan insisted it had come from the Fox costume department, but Englund wasn't buying. Cornered, Joan told the truth. Englund shaded from pique to fury and, cursing her, snatched the necklace and hurled it to the floor. It exploded in dozens of different directions, and it was several hours before all the pieces were found. Joan was mortified, of course, but she was also indignant at the hypocrisy of this two-timer criticizing *her* morals.

The two made up, but Englund got in a lather again when Joan, along with Zsa Zsa and other actresses, made headlines during a Congressional investigation to determine whether the high living of Trujillo, *père et fils*, was being funded by American aid. Englund returned to Leachman, then left again, reconciling with Joan. Then, no doubt inspired by Joan's example, he dallied openly with another woman. Joan happened to see them together, and quickly put a stop to *that* bit of intrigue, after which Englund went back to his wife. So dizzying were these events that Leachman has half joked that if she ever writes an autobiography it would have to be called *Meanwhile, Back at the Ranch*. . . .

These confrontations, Englund's inability to leave Leachman, and Joan's willingness to take him back each time he tried, caused the relationship to become its own self-parody. It would, in fact, take twenty years for Englund and Leachman to split for good, by which time Joan had long given up on him.

In the midst of all these romantic contortions, Joan was professionally unfulfilled and says, "I about went off my rocker. I'd wake up about eleven, have coffee and talk on the telephone an hour and a half," chatting with her girlfriends and poking around for word of loan-outs that might be good for her. After that, she'd go to lunch, go to singing and dancing classes which she'd begun, to stay sane, and then head for her analyst.

United Artists came calling again, interested in getting Joan for the part of a woman whose lover is torn between her and allegiance to the IRA in the James Cagney film *Shake Hands with the Devil*, but Fox didn't let her go to Ireland to make it. Skouras suddenly had a great idea for a movie, and the studio wanted Joan on the lot just in case they decided to use her. Had Joan known the frustration which lay ahead, she might well have left Fox and taken the film.

The "great idea" was a remake of a film that had been one of Fox's biggest silent movie hits, *Cleopatra*. It began in September 1958, when Skouras brought independent producer Walter Wanger to the studio to put the picture together. At the time, Wanger, Skouras, and Fox's head of production Buddy Adler felt there were two ways to go: to make a mammoth picture starring a mammoth box-office star, Elizabeth Taylor, or make a relatively small film, for no more than $1.2 million, starring Joanne Woodward, model Suzy Parker, or any of the Fox contract players who, at the time, included Joan, Dolores Michaels, Millie Perkins, and Barbara Steele.

Skouras was partial to Woodward, who had just

nabbed an Oscar for *The Three Faces of Eve;* Wanger favored Taylor, who told him in November that she'd think about it; and Adler wanted Joan.

By February 1959, Fox had not yet completed the script, Taylor was preparing to make *Suddenly Last Summer* with Katharine Hepburn and Montgomery Clift at Columbia and was thus unavailable, Woodward was determined to be not quite voluptuous enough to be the Queen of the Nile, Suzy Parker was pregnant, and the others were deemed not up to the part for reasons of experience or looks. Wanger recalls, "Adler was insistent we use Joan Collins, who was physically right for the role and was dying to play it." That she was, and for all her dislike of the panting Skouras, she, according to Skouras biographer Carlo Curti, "quietly purred in his ear that she was the one for the role." Just what this purring entailed is not known although, coincidentally, Skouras suddenly had a change of heart toward her. Apart from having the chest Skouras felt Cleopatra should possess, he liked the fact that Joan was under contract. If the film were a hit, he would have himself a star.

Joan was gleeful, though her joy faded slightly when she was turned over to Fox's dance director Hermes Pan, whose assignment, says Wanger, was to "try to improve her posture and walk so she will have the grace and dignity of Cleopatra." Joan resented this, feeling that she'd been walking just fine for years; but Fox was insistent. What's more, they were right. Joan's walk was great for a cheap queen like Nellifer, or a twentieth-century vamp, poured into a tight skirt or pants and swaying like a buoy; Cleopatra needed less swish and more *implied* power and sex appeal.

While Joan was learning how to walk, the script was being completed. When it was finished and costed-out, much to Fox's alarm the budget was determined to be nearly $3 million. The filmmakers began to get nervous. Would a relative unknown like

Joan be able to pull in enough theatergoers to make a profit, or was it better to spend an extra half-million or so and get a big box-office star?

The indecision lasted through the summer and into the fall, though as far as Joan knew the part was still hers. She went through makeup and costume tests to find the right look for Cleopatra, and also took lessons in diction so that she could speak like a queen. It was also necessary for her to lose weight, since the slinky sensuality Pan was trying to achieve cried out for slimmer lines below the bust.

By spring, Joan was screen-testing to make sure that everything from her voice to the jewelry and the togas looked right. When they didn't, it was back to the drawing board followed by further screen tests. This process dragged on through the summer and into the fall, though not all of it was due to Fox's quest for perfection. They were still anxious about Joan's being able to carry a film this big, and started talking again to Taylor, as well as to Sophia Loren, Audrey Hepburn, and Gina Lollobrigida. Scripts went out to all of them, and both Hepburn and Taylor were impressed enough to accept the part. From Skouras's point of view, there were drawbacks to both: Hepburn had no bust, and Taylor wanted a million dollars which, at the time, was an unheard-of price for an actress. The Fox president knew that while one of DeMille's Biblical epics could easily make back $4 million—which is what this film would cost with Taylor—he wasn't so certain about *Cleopatra*.

Nonetheless, Fox and Taylor came to terms in October and, after all the training and testing and hoping, Joan was sent to the showers. She admits that after years of trying not to take any of her setbacks to heart, she cried over losing the part; and though she told herself *something better will come along*, she didn't believe it. She felt as if she'd lost the role of a lifetime, though she put on a brave face in public. "Well, Elizabeth Taylor is shorter than me and doesn't walk like a queen either [but] I quite understand why it's necessary to replace me with Liz, and I accept it philosophically." In private, however, she was so very bitter that she told Associated Press with more than a touch of disgust, "In England, I used to think Hollywood was just the end of everything. I expected the whole place to look like Beverly Hills. Everybody was rich and rolled in luxury. Everywhere you looked were movie studios. Now," she shrugged, "it's just a place. It has smog and unattractive areas just like any other city."

Being a star, she was finding out, "is just a job."

Chapter Twelve

The blow of losing *Cleopatra* was blunted somewhat by having found a new boyfriend, one who would take Joan closer to the altar than she'd been since Maxwell Reed.

Early in 1959, both George Englund and *Cleopatra* were still peripheral realities in her life. Englund was again "off" with Leachman, and he and Joan were seen at various industry functions. (Columnist Earl Wilson remembers a party, which Buddy Adler gave for Ingrid Bergman in April. He recalls that when Englund dared to stray from Joan's side for a few minutes, she angrily rose and "flounced off" after him, Wilson noting with admiration, "and she can sure flounce." When she got him back, Wilson says, she stuck close to him, "kissing George's ear.")

But while Joan would monopolize and nuzzle Englund in public, the relationship had been too deeply eroded to recover. Thus, the all-or-nothing Joan was ripe for being swept off her feet yet again.

Warren Beatty was four years younger than Joan, having just turned twenty-two. Not long before, he had given up a good job as a construction worker to follow in the footsteps of his older sister, Shirley MacLaine, and become an actor. He had recently landed a continuing role in a new series called *The Many Loves of Dobie Gillis*, playing the self-impressed Milton Armitage, but it was motion pictures he wanted and, with a drive virtually unparalleled in movie history, it was motion pictures he would have.

Joan first saw Beatty while dining at La Scala or, rather, he saw her, recognizing Joan and staring at her from across the restaurant. The sighting was pure chance, for she was not high on Beatty's list of want-to-meet actresses; he had recently seen Joan in *The Bravados* and, as she tells it, "he was very disillusioned by what he saw. He came away saying I was not so hot." Spotting her at La Scala, however, he realized that the film had not showcased Joan to the best advantage.

Joan was taken with Beatty's boyish good looks, though she describes him as having been "myopic [and] and pimply-faced." They exchanged nothing but glances that day and it was several weeks before he got around to asking her to dinner. She accepted and, once again, Joan fell in love between soup and dessert. By the time they got back to her apartment, she was hooked on him.

For the next few weeks, Joan juggled Englund and Beatty before finally deciding that Beatty—mercurial, volatile, innocent, loving, ambitious, sincere and, perhaps most important, really and truly available— was better suited to her. She made the break with Englund outside her psychiatrist's office, where they happened to meet. It hurt her, it hurt him, and he protested; but when he saw that Joan was determined, he pulled himself erect, professed his love, and watched her walk out of his life.

When Joan and *Cleopatra* parted company, Fox gave her a mediocre consolation prize: *Seven Thieves*, a caper film about an attempt to rob the gambling vaults in Monte Carlo. Joan took the part without a fuss only because she got to play a stripper, a profession far removed from her experience and one which she found fascinating. What's more, for several hours a day during the three weeks prior to filming she was taught the art of taking off her clothes for men—something which, apart from its practical applications, would help flush away the unpleasant remnants of the queenly gait she'd mastered.

Joan's teacher was a professional stripper named Candy Barr, who, shortly after she finished with Joan, went to prison on a narcotics charge. Joan found that stripping took far more concentration, stamina, and finesse than she had imagined. She came away with a healthy respect for the profession, which was healthier than the respect she had for Fox. Much to Joan's dismay, they wouldn't let Candy "teach me bumps and grinds . . . because the studio was afraid of the censors." Furthermore, she found it ludicrous to go through even these watered-down moves only to "strip down to something which looks like a bathing suit," another concession to the censors. When all was said and done, about the only positive things she could say about the experience were that she got to act with Edward G. Robinson and that she was, at least, "the only woman in the cast." Otherwise, she'd just about had it with the studio and their second-rate pictures. "I only have two more years with Fox," she told a reporter with the *New York Post*, "and I'm not unhappy at all about that. In fact, you may say I look forward to the day."

By this time, Fox was beginning to feel the same. Upon completing *Seven Thieves* in November, Fox put her into *Sons and Lovers*, based on D. H. Lawrence's autobiographical novel about a young man who grows discontented with his life in a mining town and tries to get out. Joan's part, as one of his girlfriends, was decidedly secondary; but the script was literate and the film would be prestigious, shot on location in Nottingham, England, and at Pinewood.

Joan, however, refused to do it.

She was in New York doing pubicity for *Seven Thieves* when she announced her decision, claiming that she was troubled by the secondary nature of the part. Her declaration took Fox by surprise. Having known that there was little that could be done with the role, given the nature of the story, she had nonetheless gone ahead and done the wardrobe and makeup tests—hardly something she'd have done if she felt so strongly about not making the movie. For her part, however, Joan insisted that Fox had promised "certain changes would be made. The role is a blah-nothing part, and I've done so many of them. The studio was certainly aware that it was a moot point all along as to whether or not I would do it. I was waiting to see the final script, and they knew it." She added that this was a long time in coming, that she was "sick of being modest. As an actress I'm very good—it's just the parts I have had [that are] unsuitable. I could be a really top box-office star if I were allowed to pick my own roles."

Upon hearing that she'd left the project, Joan's family was no less taken aback than the studio. Upon Joan's announcement, Jackie said from London that as of two weeks before, her sister had been eagerly looking forward to coming over, not having seen her family in a year. "I know she wants to come home for Christmas," she said, adding innocently, "and I am sure there are no personal attachments to keep her in New York."

That was true, strictly speaking: Warren Beatty was

in Washington, D.C., rehearsing what was to be a short-lived run of a new William Inge play called *A Loss of Roses*. After she finished her duties in New York, Joan hurried down to meet him. The truth was that regardless of the size of the part in *Sons and Lovers*, and however strongly she felt about her wells of untapped talent, Joan passed up the film because she didn't want to be an ocean away from Beatty, nor Beatty from her. Indeed, following this incident and others like it, an unnamed Fox executive would confess to a reporter from the New York *World-Telegram & Sun*, "When Joan is in love she simply takes off and to hell with her work, her career and her studio."

Joan has never denied that; however, as one who was becoming more and more dependent on astrology, she defended herself by saying, "I'm a Gemini, and I'm supposed to have many moods—and I do. One half of me loves the high life and bright lights while the other is nauseated by them."

But that was a weak rationale for what really amounted to a very short attention span. Beatty, as Englund before him, and everyone from Loew to Reed before him, was a flash of excitement. She'd grown to "hate and detest routine," tired of knowing exactly what was going to happen to her the next hour, the next day, the next week, the next month. The makeup, the costuming, the sitting around for hours while lights, sets, and cameras were adjusted, the promotional chores and photo sessions. Even if the scripts were good, it all had what to Joan was a stultifying sameness to it. She thrived on excitement, and in that sense men were almost as good as music. And Beatty was as fine a specimen of the breed as any she had ever encountered.

The response from Fox was swift and predictable. They suspended Joan again and found a replacement, having to write off the nearly $30,000 they'd spent on her wardrobe, makeup and, finally, the delays.

This suspension, like the previous one, lasted for eight weeks, the duration of filming. And when it ended, the last laugh was on Joan. Mary Ure, the actress who took her place, was Oscar-nominated for her work in *Sons and Lovers*, a performance which Joan could surely have given; also nominated were Trevor Howard for best actor, Jack Cardiff for director, the screenwriters, the sets, the cinematography (it won), and the film itself for best picture of the year. Had Joan made *Sons and Lovers*, it would have been a feather in her cap and given her far more leverage regarding whatever she did next. Instead, having bitched in public about what turned out to be an Oscar-nominated screenplay, Joan had managed only to look foolish and irresponsible.

'I've never planned anything in my life and look at all that's happened to me."

Joan tried to suggest that she always manages to land on her feet, but her decision to boycott *Sons and Lovers* hurt her not only professionally but personally as well, since for the first time since she'd left London she hadn't the money to visit her family. The only silver lining in a very dark cloud was Beatty, although Joan might have felt differently had she known, then, that at least a *part* of her appeal was that she got a lot of press and, by association, so did he. If not quite an opportunist, Beatty *was* an ambitious young man.

After the failure of *A Loss of Roses*, the couple returned to New York, where they passed the bulk of Joan's suspension. They stayed with friends as often as possible to cut down on expenses, returning to Los Angeles toward the end of February. They set up housekeeping at a small studio apartment in a hotel near Sunset Boulevard, Beatty immediately sniffing around for a movie project while Joan agreed to do a Fox western, *Big River, Big Man*. Despite her feeling that women didn't belong in westerns, she felt more

The Many Sides of Joan Collins

Joan in 1983 at age 50

Heartbreaker

First husband
Maxwell Reed (1951)

AP/WIDE WORLD PHOTOS

Joan and Sidney Chaplin
(1954)

AP/WIDE WORLD PHOTOS

Arthur Loew (1957)

Warren Beatty and Joan
(1961)

Joan with
Robert Wagner (1961)

AP/WIDE WORLD PHOTOS

Harry Belafonte

UPI/BETTMANN ARCHIVE

Joan and second
husband, Anthony Newley

Wedding picture of Joan and third spouse, Ron Kass (1972)

Ryan O'Neal

Peter Holm with Joan in 1983

AP/WIDE WORLD PHOTOS

Land of the Pharaohs (1955)

UPI/BETTMANN ARCHIVE

Joan with Evelyn Nesbit during shooting of *The Girl in the Red Velvet Swing* (1955)

Gregory Peck and Joan during *The Bravados* (1958)

Tales From the Crypt (1972)

Sir John Gielgud and Joan
during *Tales From the
Unexpected* (1978)

Joan during press
conference for *The Bitch*
(1978)

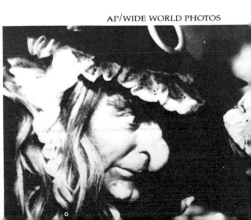

Joan as the evil
witch in *Hansel
and Gretel* on "Fairy
Tale Theatre" (1984)

"Dynasty's" Linda Evans and Joan

Joan as Alexis Carrington

The famous Cinzano ad

AP/WIDE WORLD PHOTOS

UPI/BETTMANN ARCHIVE

Joan and sister
Jackie

Joan with son, Sacha and daughter, Tara (1972)

AP/WIDE WORLD PHOTOS

Daughter Katy with Joan (1983)

Sacha and Joan (1983)

AP/WIDE WORLD PHOTOS

AP/WIDE WORLD PHOTOS

Publicity shot taken during *Island in the Sun* (1957)

Joan at age 21

AP/WIDE WORLD PHOTOS

Joan comes clean in
Rally 'Round the Flag, Boys (1958)

Joan dries
off in the highly
publicized Cannon ad

AP/WIDE WORLD PHOTOS

AP/WIDE WORLD PHOTOS

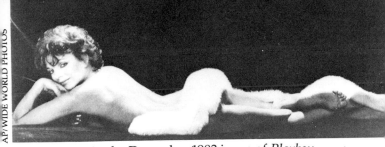

Joan poses in the December 1983 issue of *Playboy*

Joan, at 50, in *Harper's Bazaar*

Another shot from the notorious 10-page *Playboy* spread in December 1983

strongly that *this* woman shouldn't be on the unemployment line, and went to work. This time, however, Fox pulled the plug during preproduction, and Joan was once again idle. They also tried to get her into *Madison Avenue* but, encouraged by the Svengalian Beatty, Joan showed her claws and turned the unexciting advertising "expose" down. This time she was right since the script was so bad that even Fox delayed the project for rethinking.

The couple spent a lot of time in bed, which was just about Beatty's favorite place to be. One of his later paramours, Britt Ekland, would say of him that he was "the most divine lover of all. His libido was as lethal as high octane gas. I had never known such pleasure and passion in my life." Joan agrees that Beatty often left her exhausted because of his extraordinary sexual appetite—although he frequently admonished her that she would be in better shape both physically *and* mentally if she would adopt his healthful regimen of exercise, all-natural foods, scads of vitamins, and also give up smoking, a habit he detested. But Joan was too set in her nonsportive, nicotine-craving, dessert-loving ways; besides, she needed those indulgences to help her relax when the going got tough. Beatty could channel his frustrations into professional pursuits—phoning agents, producers, writers, directors, and fellow actors in search of tips or leads, which he did for hours each day—but Joan tended to internalize pressure. Her vices were like a balm which got inside and numbed the pain.

One crisis neither Joan nor Beatty could handle by their tried-and-true methods was the matter of Joan's pregnancy. When Joan got the word, the couple were just preparing to go to New York, where Elia Kazan would be directing *Splendor in the Grass*. Thanks to a combination of bravura, hard sell, and the aggressive support of screenwriter Inge, Beatty had landed the starring role; however, looking at Joan's dazed expression and listening to what she had to say brought his exhilaration crashing to earth.

Possessed with a kind of numb horror, both knew, from the start, what had to be done. Marriage was out of the question: she and Beatty were both too career-oriented. Having the baby was not an option: unwed mothers were frowned upon in 1960, and Fox would certainly have tossed her out by invoking the morals clause in her contract. That in itself wouldn't have been disastrous, but it would have made Joan persona non grata throughout Hollywood. Nor could she have put a child of hers up for adoption, spending the rest of her life wondering where it was and whether or not it was happy.

The actress had known other girls who had had abortions, from RADA to Beverly Hills. At worst, a bungled operation could kill the woman or leave her sterile; and she suspected that even a successful abortion would leave emotional scars. However, objectionable as it was, it was the only course open to them.

Beatty called a friend in New York who, as it turned out, knew someone that would do the job safely and professionally. An appointment was made, they flew east for the film and, a day later, the deed was done. Life resumed a semblance of normalcy: Beatty went to work rehearsing and Joan made ready to fly to Rome to make what was to be her last film for Fox. Despite the tears she shed whenever she thought about the abortion, life went on. However, she was starting to see that in life prosperity wasn't really the thing to aspire to: if one just managed to *survive*, she should be grateful. That was an important realization, for "high octane" Mr. Beatty, among others, was about to give Joan some of the rockiest times of her life.

Chapter Thirteen

Joan once set an ideal life-style for herself. If she could order events to her liking, she said she'd spend early summer in the South of France, late summer in the West Indies, autumn in New York, winter in Southern California, and spring in either London, Paris, or Rome.

Rome, Joan says, is among her favorite cities. It has history and culture the way London does, only more so; it has the beauty of Paris and it has Italian men—romance!

Before leaving Los Angeles, Joan was told to report to Rome for a new picture, *Esther and the King*. Set in the fourth century B.C., the film is about the Persian King Ahasuerus and his love for the Judean girl Esther, who uses her wiles to try to dissuade him from persecuting the Jews. Ordinarily, it would have been a part to which the half-Jewish Joan might have cottoned; as it was, her lack of enthusiasm was great. The script was pedestrian, much of the cast was Italian and spoke *only* Italian; their voices would be dubbed later, meaning that they and the few English-speaking players wouldn't understand each other during their scenes together. Joan's leading man was Richard Egan who, at thirty-nine, was considered a second-stringer and, moreover, she would be away from Beatty for several months. That Joan was the top-billed star of the film, and would be in her favorite city, failed miserably to compensate for the rest of it.

One of the biggest annoyances was that her fame brought out the infamous paparazzi. "They're like something out of *La Dolce Vita*," she grumbled. "They're all young kids in their early teens or twenties and they don't work for anyone—they only get money if they sell their pictures to some magazine. So they like to aggravate people, goad them, to get an expressive picture. They trail me down the Via Veneto, so I say, 'Okay, I'll pose for a picture,' and I do, but they don't go away. They snicker and laugh and goad you and follow you on their Vespas. It's impossible to go out in Rome without them finding you." Thus, Joan couldn't even enjoy the night life, which was a bother. She didn't like sitting in her hotel room now any more than she had in the past, though as the weeks dragged on, she became more restless than usual because of some long-distance problems with Beatty.

In August, not long before her departure, Joan and Beatty had become engaged. He'd proposed to her in a way that was pure, iconoclastic Beatty: he buried the ring in some chopped liver where she would find it. This was, in all likelihood, a wry send-up of the way Robert Wagner had proposed to Beatty's *Splendor in the Grass* co-star, Natalie Wood, by slipping her a ring in a crystal champagne glass filled with Dom Perignon. Romance was not one of Beatty's virtues. But Joan overlooked that and accepted, and they set the wedding date for January 1961.

One of Beatty's historic problems where women are concerned is his notoriously brief attention span. Says Hollywood sex chronicler Shirley Sealy, "His reputation as one of Hollywood's great hit-and-run swingers has few parallels since Errol Flynn first went to play," and it was not long into production of *Splendor in the Grass* that he cast his eye on Natalie Wood. Though she had been married to Robert Wagner for just over two and one-half years, their relationship was strained. Her career was on the rise while Wagner was fast being eclipsed by stars like Steve McQueen, Paul Newman, and Beatty. The result was jealousy and tension, which Natalie handled by turning off to Wagner.

Confused and lonely, Natalie was immediately impressed by Beatty, who was dynamic and aggressive and didn't let the system push him around the way Wagner did. Though Natalie did not want to hurt Joan, being with Beatty was akin to a religious experience. Oddly enough, she happened to complement him far better than his fiancée. Joan and Beatty had the same drive, biting wit, irreverence, and unwillingness to be bossed or manhandled. When they were locked arm in arm and standing against Hollywood, they were indomitable; but when they turned on each other, it was a different story.

The intensity of the Beatty-Collins battles dwarfed anything Joan had experienced before, especially when she traveled from Rome to New York for a weekend visit. Beatty would write or call and tell Joan how much he missed her, and she would hurry over—never vice versa, since *he* was making "art" and his input was vital, whereas she was just muddling through a warmed-over Biblical epic. As soon as she got there, he would accuse her of having an affair and they would fight throughout her stay. Whether or not Joan really did have an affair with any of her co-stars when she first went to Rome (which is doubtful, given the loyalty she shows a lover until he hurts her), she would have had every reason to jump into a Trujillo-like fling as the weeks progressed, by which time he was actively pursuing Natalie Wood. In Beatty's book, it was okay for him to make a fool of Joan behind her back, but not all right for her to do the same.

Joan kept flying over to see him, destroying her credibility in Rome but holding up her part of the relationship. She defended her actions on a creative level by stating, "I've been in more truly awful films than anyone else in history. So how can you be dedicated when you know you're making rubbish?" But her colleagues on *Esther and the King* were trying hard, and they felt she should too. As a result, her behavior alienated the crew and totally disgusted Raoul Walsh, the director, who suspended her three times. The first time, his inclination was to replace her, but that would have meant scrapping everything he'd already shot. Instead, Walsh decided to struggle through, saving scenes that did not involve her for whenever she took off, and removing her from the payroll while she was gone.

Joan's worst fears for *Esther and the King* came to pass. "It was dreadful," she said upon seeing the film at the end of the year, though most critics felt she was being charitable. As for her efforts to please Beatty, they were only slightly more successful. By January 1961 the marriage had been postponed for a few weeks; by March, it was postponed indefinitely, ostensibly because Beatty was on a new film. "Both of us like long engagements," she told Bob Thomas at Associated Press. "I once got married fast and it was a disaster." But she had begun to sense that Beatty didn't want to get married, that he had proposed out of a sense of obligation for her months of support and, perhaps, out of regret for the emotional strain she'd suffered because of the abortion.

March was significant in another way, for it more or less ended her six-year relationship with Fox. Early in the month, Joan got a call from her agent that a new Cleopatra might be needed at any moment: Elizabeth Taylor had come down with staphylococcus pneumonia and was in very bad shape. Though an emergency tracheotomy had been performed to open her windpipe so she could breathe, and she was on an automatic respirator, the eleven doctors attending her did not believe she would survive.

As much as Joan still yearned to play Cleopatra, she did not want it this way. For its part, Fox really didn't want her, but they couldn't afford to shut the picture down: *Cleopatra* had already cost $5 million, the forty-odd insurance companies involved with the film weren't prepared to write if off, and Fox was thus committed to spending another $5 million to finish it (though that figure would balloon to a whopping $40 million before they were through). From March 3 to March 6, Taylor fought to survive; throughout that period, Joan stayed by the phone dreading the call that would summon her to London to replace her friend. Finally, late on March 6, the actress began to show slight signs of improvement and, displaying remarkable resilience, was out of danger by the ninth.

Joan and Cleopatra were *finally* through, and she was once again inactive. She campaigned for a part in a comedy, "trying unsuccessfuly to convince them that that was what I wanted to do," but they turned her down. That hurt, because she knew "the trend was toward comedy, and there were no young comediennes to match the great ones of the thirties and forties, like Jean Arthur, Claudette Colbert, Rosalind Russell and Carole Lombard. I wanted a chance."

Angry and exasperated, she decided to negotiate her departure from the studio, which, as it turned out, Fox was willing to do. Caught in the bottomless pit of *Cleopatra*, they were looking to cut overhead and agreed to let Joan go. In exchange for the freedom to accept outside film offers, they asked only that she agree to make two films for them at some future date.

Joan was elated. "I used to promise myself I'd never make any more trash," she said, "but I always did. Well, now it's different. I'm interested in my career, but I'm also interested in being happy. If I can't do good films, I'll go and sell socks in a department store."

For a while, it looked like she might have to do just that. In May she agreed to a three-picture deal with Columbia, the first film of which was to be *The War Lover*, with Joan as an RAF WAAF who falls in love with Steve McQueen. But the pact fell through, Joan later saying of this period, "My reputation for being a bit of a swinger did harm my career. They all thought I was more interested in dating than in acting." Instead of working, Joan spent May with Beatty in Rome and London where he was shooting *The Roman Spring of Mrs. Stone*, based on the novel by Tennessee Williams. She tried not to think of what may have gone on between the actor and Natalie—and now with his co-star Vivien Leigh, not to mention actress Susan Strasberg (with whom he actually moved in while Joan was away, one time seducing her in a bathroom at the home of director Luchino Visconti during a party). When Joan and Beatty were in London, she didn't even bother to stay with him in his rented house, but lived with her parents in another part of town. The couple were together often, but not always; she preferred spending time with her mother, who had recently undergone surgery for a tumor and had not managed to regain her former good health.

While she was in London, Joan heard that filmmakers Norman Panama and Melvin Frank were planning to make another "Road" picture with Bob Hope and Bing Crosby, this one entitled *The Road to Hong Kong*. Joan remembers, "I had seen *The Facts of Life* [starring Hope and directed by Frank] and I thought it was one of the funniest films I'd seen in years. I called them and said I would love to be in the picture." The filmmakers were reluctant because they knew Joan only as a dramatic actress, and she got a typical Hollywood stall: "They said it was too early to discuss casting, but they would let me know later." Joan was unwilling to let it go at that, and when she got back to Los Angeles she arranged a screening of

Rally 'Round the Flag, Boys! "They liked me in it," she says, "and I got the part."

Since *Road to Hong Kong* was being made in London in August, it would necessitate being away from Beatty. By that time, however, it really didn't matter. They were fighting constantly. Beatty's snobbish quest for art made him irascible, and continuing suspicions of infidelity had driven a wedge between them. Add to that Joan's belief that "people who are creative have more emotional problems than most others," and they both knew there was no reason to continue hanging on. Joan went to London and Beatty took up with Natalie Wood, who by this time had divorced Wagner—something which her relationship with Beatty allegedly accelerated.

When it was all over, Joan felt used. Her support, both emotional and financial, had helped Beatty get a leg up; now that she had outlived her usefulness, it was on to a bigger star. It's unlikely Beatty fell for Natalie as hard as she'd fallen for him. He enjoyed her, but she was a useful entrée into exclusive Hollywood circles and greater press coverage, both of which Beatty wanted. (She was, for example, Beatty's ticket into the 1961 Academy Awards, where her film *West Side Story* was competing, and photographs of the couple appeared everywhere.) That relationship, too, would quickly expire, and Beatty would move in succession to Leslie Caron, Britt Ekland, Anjelica Huston, Michelle Phillips, Barbra Streisand, Julie Christie, and Diane Keaton, among countless others. He felt, says Susan Strasberg, a "tremendous need to please women as well as conquer them," after which, once they outlived their usefulness, they were discarded.

So Joan had been tossed aside. What was worse, her devotion to Beatty had cost her an Oscar-nominated film and all but destroyed her credibility as a dedicated actress. It was time to start rebuilding.

Chapter Fourteen

❖❖❖❖❖❖❖❖❖❖❖❖❖❖❖❖❖❖❖❖❖❖❖❖❖❖❖❖❖❖❖❖❖❖❖❖❖

Road to Hong Kong was the seventh of the "Road" pictures, following roads to Singapore, Zanzibar, Morocco, Utopia, Rio, and Bali. In all, Bob Hope and Bing Crosby were usually down-and-out characters looking for a quick buck, and becoming embroiled in schemes that ultimately backfired. This last "Road" picture was no exception. The stars portrayed a pair of con artists who become involved with a spy (Joan) who is searching for stolen plans to a rocket that will give her people—who happen to live underwater!—access to the planet Plutonius and tap its stores of the valuable element plutonium. "None of it makes any sense," Joan admits, but she adds, "It's not supposed to, with Hope and Crosby around."

Though she was not, in fact, wildly excited by the nonsensical story line, Joan was very glad to have the part. In August, just before shooting began, she said, "I've already worked with Bob on a TV show, and I've met Bing. I know I'm going to have a ball. My only worry is that I'll break up so often that they'll have to fire me." She was also thrilled to be wearing "very sleek, high fashions in the picture" and, despite all the unpleasant memories attached to Rank, it was good to be back in London, at Shepperton, with her family. Just about the only thing she definitely did *not* enjoy was being back where the English press could get at her. She had bitter memories of the way they'd lambasted her for all her tarts performances, and things had gotten worse while she was away. "They hate me," she said. "That generally happens to English performers who go to America." As a result, she refused to give local reporters any interviews. They called her arrogant and worse, but Joan didn't care. They'd have said that even if she'd talked with them, so at least she wouldn't make it worse by giving them the opportunity to twist her words around or take them out of context. She also didn't want to have to answer questions about Beatty or about Robert Wagner who, ironically, was in London shooting *The War Lover* and whom she dated now and then. The press wanted to make something sordid about Natalie's "ex-" seeing Joan while *her* "ex-" was busy with Natalie, and she did not want to encourage such speculation by granting interviews.

Road to Hong Kong passed pleasantly, Joan having as much fun as she'd anticipated acting with Hope, though the dour Crosby was a disappointment. Overall, she was satisfied with the work she'd done and felt that the film would be a big hit and would help her get into other comedies. Even while the film was in production she was planning to option a few properties and get them produced herself—convinced, as she'd said before, that she knew best the kinds of roles that would make her a star. However, while *Road to Hong Kong* was indeed a box-office smash, Joan would not work again for another two years. This time the culprit wasn't a tyrannical studio putting her on suspension or failing to come up with properties. This time, as before, the cause was Joan's habit of falling madly and totally in love.

The object of her affection was singer/writer/actor Anthony Newley, whom she met while shooting *Road to Hong Kong*. It came about this way: "A mate of both of us, dancer Joyce Blair, came down to Shepperton Studios to have lunch with me," recalls Joan. "She was talking about this new musical *Stop the World—I Want to Get Off* which had just opened in the West

End. She was astonished to hear I'd never met Newley before. 'But you *must* meet him,' she said. 'I've known him since we were kids, and you must be *mad* if you haven't seen his musical.'

"On the way home from filming that night, Joyce and I went round to his flat, but he wasn't there. Either it was a matinee day, when he always stayed on between shows, or else he had just gone to the theater early, as he often did, to absorb the atmosphere of the stage before starting the evening performance."

Joan continues, "So Joyce arranged that she should bring him down to Shepperton for lunch, and while he was there he invited me to see the show, which had only been open for about three weeks. I can remember the exact day I first saw it because it was the day Jackie's first child was born, September 4."

During their lunch, Joan was enchanted but not smitten by Newley. He was not as refined as the men to whom Joan was accustomed and, worse, he was English, which, to Joan's way of thinking, was an automatic turnoff since she'd been burned by Englishmen before. On top of that, she says, "His hair wasn't long enough and his clothes—well, they didn't fit him. They were baggy." At five feet ten inches, he was also a little shorter than she liked her men.

But he did have a wacky sense of humor and a joie de vivre, both of which Warren Beatty lacked, and though she only told Joyce that she was "impressed" with him, she was delighted when he invited her to come and see the show. Since she hadn't regarded Newley as anything more than a potential friend, she invited Robert Wagner to be her escort. When the show was over, the three of them went to dinner.

Dinner was much more fun than lunch had been, the three of them drinking and laughing, though Wagner must have felt just a little like a third leg when the two Britons reminisced about what it was like to grow up during the war, and how England had changed in Joan's absence. In fact, says Newley, "I had a problem. I was intrigued with Joan and wondered how I could get rid of her date."

For Newley, the witty, vivacious Joan was a welcome respite from what had literally been a lifetime of overwork and hardship. Two years older than she, Newley was haunted by memories of a lonely childhood. Among his most vivid recollections are being bused out of London to escape the bombing. Unlike Joan, who lived with her family, Newley had his name pinned to his shirt and was given over to a succession of families who were paid $2 a week to shelter him. "A sense of abandonment set in," he says, "and I've always had to fight it." He didn't go home after the war and drifted into acting at the age of fourteen when, working as an office boy to earn school tuition, he was spotted by a director and hired to appear in the film *The Adventures of Dusty Bates*. Newley followed that with *The Little Ballerina* and *Oliver Twist*, in which he played the Artful Dodger. For the next thirteen years, Newley labored in a total of forty-three films although, like Joan, he was frustrated at the way stardom constantly eluded him.

In 1956, Newley married actress Anne Lynn and they had a baby boy, who died shortly after his birth. According to Newley's longtime friend and collaborator, Leslie Bricusse, "The shock to Tony was tremendous, and may have spoiled the marriage. He buried himself in work and produced and produced. But personally he was lost, given to extremes." Separating from Lynn in 1958, Newley holed up with Bricusse and turned out the book and music for *Stop the World—I Want to Get Off*, the Everyman saga of Littlechap and how he deals with the triumphs and setbacks of life.

The success of the play did not make Newley a star of the caliber he'd always wanted. But its songs, "What Kind of Fool Am I?," "Once in a Lifetime," and "Gonna Build a Mountain" were so widely

recorded that it guaranteed him a hefty annual
income for life, and he was certainly the man of the
hour in the West End—confident his fortunes would
increase even more when he took the show to New
York.

Apart from being a lively and appreciative companion for Joan, Newley was one thing more. All of the
men whom Joan had lived with or dated extensively
were talented and charismatic; none, however, was a
genius. Newley was that, using song and drama to
pinpoint not just his own demons but those in
society; he was not a Beatty, who merely envisioned
himself an *artiste* and wore the appropriate airs. Joan
recognized his talent and was so awed by it that she
became a worshiper at the shrine, something to
which Newley couldn't help but respond.

Because Elsa's health had begun to deteriorate,
Joan stayed on in London after *Road to Hong Kong*.
Jackie was married and had her hands full with a
child, so Joan spent the next few months caring for
her mother and commiserating with her father because they would soon lose her. Joe was a softer man
than the one she had known for years, and Joan was
concerned about how he would fare after Elsa's
death.

Toward the end of March 1962, Joan reluctantly left
London to spend ten days in New York promoting
Road to Hong Kong. There, while her mother lay
dying, she was forced to say interesting things about
a film she considered "terribly commercial and great
escapist entertainment," but was otherwise nothing
to crow about. She spent time ducking questions
about Warren Beatty, being asked her opinion of the
Liz Taylor–Richard Burton headlines ("I'm [not] an
expert on extramarital affairs," she'd say evasively),
and defending her past.

So that she wouldn't get lonely, Newley had
thoughtfully given her a traveling companion, a
poodle she named Ladybird. As expected, Joan spent

a lot of time grooming her so that she wouldn't be "such a scruffy-looking mutt" while being walked among "all the chic Park Avenue dogs." Joan also spent a lot of time with friends, in ten days managing to go to six discothèques, where she expressed her passion for the Twist, as well as taking in seven plays.

Returning to London, Joan saw a lot of Newley, both in bed as well as out. Since she knew she was falling in love with him, Joan made certain early on to "come clean" about her past. She told him everything, she says, "determined he was not going to find out anything about me from anyone else." His ready acceptance of her impetuous acts and often questionable ethics made her love him even more. "A lot of men's egos can't take the fact that their women have been with other men," she says admiringly, "which shows a lack of security in their masculinity. Tony's not like that."

When they went out, more often than not Joan and Newley double-dated with Leslie and Yvonne Bricusse, both of whom were intelligent and delightful, not to mention being devoted friends. Newley was completely open and at ease with them, which was important when the pressures of doing what was fundamentally a one-man show got to him; moreover, it was the kind of friendship where Joan didn't feel as though she was intruding when Newley was working and it was just she and the Bricusses at dinner, a movie, or simply sitting around. (She did, however, have to put the brakes on the good food since she gained ten pounds immediately after finishing *Road to Hong Kong*. It was her inclination to be chubby and, feeling that Sophia Loren was the only person on whom "big" was "chic," she became very diligent about watching her weight.)

Joan didn't realize it at the time, but her attraction to Newley was based on more than just the scope of his talent. When Elsa died in May 1962, she did so convinced that her daughter, in Joan's words, "would

come to a bad end because I was a little bit wild."
Subconsciously, Joan had to feel that Newley was a
way to satisfy her mother, both in her final days and
"in spirit." He was an anchor, a source of respectability; and he was someone with whom to build a family.
Not that he was flawless, as Joan quickly learned. He
was moody and temperamental, but at least it was
because of genius and not affectation. He also tended
to be cold at times, though not vindictive, and he
could, on the other hand, be very, very loving. It
remains one of Joan's greatest sorrows that her
mother never got to see her turn out "better than she
had estimated."

Joan left London during the summer, since Newley
was totally preoccupied with filming *The Small World
of Sammy Lee*, cutting records, dabbling with a new
play, and getting ready to take *Stop the World—I Want
to Get Off* to Broadway. She returned to Los Angeles,
renting a house, expecting to be there several months
while she fulfilled her contractual obligations to Fox.
The agreement they'd signed specified that she had
to do a picture for them by June or the studio would
have to pay her. However, because they were devot-
ing so much money and attention to *Cleopatra*, the
studio couldn't come up with anything and Joan
ended up killing time yet again.

No matter. The last few months had been an
onslaught of deeply felt emotions, from profound
sorrow to elation, and she could use the time to settle
down. As it turned out, she needed the respite.
When Newley and the play came over in September,
she entered a period of emotional extremes which
would make 1962 seem like a lark.

Chapter Fifteen

◆◆◆

*B*efore going to Broadway, *Stop the World—I Want to Get Off* spent time in Philadephia, ironing out the kinks for the American audience. It opened there September 17, with the Broadway debut slated for October 4, 1962.

Joan flew to Philadelphia to be with Newley and the Bricusses where, completely without warning or foreshadowing, Newley dropped a bombshell: he was carrying on with one of the actresses in the show. He was apologetic, he wasn't sure whether or not he loved the girl, but he admitted that in any case she appealed to him. His confession was like a dash of cold water, but Joan took it stoically, packing her bags and heading back to the coast. Before leaving, however, she promised to be at the New York premiere, out of respect for the friendship she'd shared with Newley and the Bricusses for nearly a year. Though she cried for another lost love, she honestly didn't feel jealous or wish Newley ill. He may have been physically unfaithful to her, but intellectually he was as devoted as ever to his *real* love—his work. Now that she had stepped back from the relationship, Joan realized that he had probably never been hers; pain and disappointment she felt, but jealousy, no.

Back in her rented house, Joan felt very much alone. Her mother was gone, and the man she'd hoped to marry was also gone. Hollywood suddenly seemed more isolated than ever, and she began to consider offers to make movies in Rome. She was totally free once again, except, of course, from her memories, her disappointment at having lived twenty-nine years without a home, a man's devotion, or even a truly good film to show for it. "The publicity makes me seem a creature living for today, wildly searching for pleasure," she said. After a dramatic pause she continued, "Baloney—to put it politely."

Joan was close to signing a deal to make a picture when she flew east for Newley's Broadway debut. She made a point of dating actor Terence Stamp while she was in New York. Stamp, a brooding Englishman, was handsome in a plain way, with intense eyes and an ascetic manner. Nothing could have come of it, Stamp's interests lying in abstract thinking and philosophy, which were not Joan's forte. However, she clearly didn't date Stamp with an eye on the future but on the present, obviously wanting to go tit-for-tat with Newley, to hurt him by suggesting that he was not worth pining over.

But that was not, alas, how Joan felt. The New York critics might hate Newley, lambasting him and the show as heavy-handed—though the music had presold it and audiences made *Stop the World—I Want to Get Off* a hit—but she could not hate him. As she watched the show yet again, his endearing, long-suffering, vulnerable stage persona reminded her of those same qualities in Newley himself. Thus, when he asked to see her just to talk, she agreed—warily, since he could ingratiate himself to anyone and he had hurt her. But she was still looking for the kind of domesticity she'd envisioned back in London, and when they sat down in Central Park Newley was *so* sincere. He said he wanted to have a relationship, and so, Joan admitted, did she; her only stipulation was that he have it with her. Newley conceded the point and they went from there, finally agreeing to marry as soon as he could obtain a divorce.

"I vowed to change," Newley says with characteristic conviction. "One of my problems has alway been communicating what I'd call that crashing intensity of mine to other people. Gradually, I suppose, you learn that you *must* relax."

For her part, Joan agreed to be slightly less of an idealist. "Everything in the movies is simply lovely. Only in time do you know that no one is perfect and only then you can love people for their faults. Otherwise, when the rough trouble comes, you can't weather the storm."

In April 1963, Newley's attorney took to court confessions of adultery signed by both Newley and Joan. Though they hardly made a secret of their relationship—they appeared at the Tony Awards that month, by which time Joan was already four months pregnant—the documents made for some embarrassing headlines. But it was the only way to expedite Newley's divorce from his wife Anne, so they put up with headlines like "NEWLEY & JOAN ADMIT ALL" and STOP THE WORLD—MRS. ANTHONY NEWLEY IS CALLING IT QUITS." Newley didn't handle the momentary infamy particularly well, brushing off reporters and acting sullen. The divorce was granted on April 23 and, getting out of the spotlight, on May 27 Joan and Newley drove an hour into neighboring Connecticut to marry.

They were already living together in Newley's plush, $1,150-a-month apartment at the Imperial House, on Sixty-ninth Street and Lexington Avenue, so the marriage didn't change anything. Newley was absorbed with the show, and Joan had thrown herself "into things like decorating," setting up a nursery, and doing all she could to prepare for motherhood. "I had never really imagined that I *would* have a baby," she says, "and so I learned as much about it as I could. I went to the public library and read about how women went through childbirth two or three hundred years ago, then I had a course in natural childbirth—muscle exercises and the right kind of breathing and all that." It would be years before that became fashionable (in motherhood as in romance, Joan was always ahead of her time), but she was determined to give her new family every bit of care and attention she could muster. Then, too, the abortion had run roughshod over her motherly instincts. That was by no means forgotten, and it strenghtened her resolve to do this right.

Preoccupied with the impending birth, Joan didn't really miss her career. The prospect of staying put for more than a few months was a refreshing change. After years of moving from apartment to rented home back to apartment, it was good to be able to unpack the "stacks of stuff in storage," and she says it was "like Christmas" finding all the things she owned, including a total of fifteen toasters she'd managed to accumulate over the years.

"We didn't enter into our marriage lightly," Joan said later. "It was part of our agreement, and our desire and our need, that Tony be there as fathers should be, for the delivery of the child."

Thus, on October 12, 1963, Newley missed the Saturday matinee to be with Joan when, at 1:58, she gave birth to Tara Cynara Newley. Joan was in heaven, set to nurse the baby and feeling a real purpose for the first time in years. In fact, she was "so thrilled with the whole thing" that she wrote an article for a woman's magazine about the experience. However, Newley's reaction was curious. An illegitimate child who never knew his father, he was glad to be a parent, but anxious because he had no role model and, further, was in a rather odd profession. "How am I going to be a good father to you?" he asked, bending over his daughter. "What will you think when Mummy brings you to the theater and you see Daddy in a hairnet, making up?" He later wrote a song about what a pity it was that the most

important job in the world, raising each new generation, is left to amateurs.

As soon as the baby was born, the Newleys hired a
nurse, not only to leave less of the rearing to chance
but because, Joan said, "I want to be both a wife and
a mother without slighting either area. I have both
instincts and they aren't incompatible." Accordingly,
life was orderly chaos for a few weeks, Newley doing
six evening shows a week plus matinees with one day
off, while Joan enjoyed a life of relative ease, now and
them going to the theater and primarily just taking
care of Tara and "watching her grow up," which she
found "the most fascinating thing in the world
because [she] does something different every day."
One of those "different" things was being made to
swear, at the age of three weeks, that she was not a
member of the Communist Party. Although Tara was
an American citizen by virtue of her birth, her parents
were English, making it necessary to affirm her
allegiance to this country. Joan and Newley did the
actual swearing, finding the entire process somewhat
ludicrous.

By November, Newley was feeling little of the
contentment Joan was experiencing. He felt he was
stagnating, for one thing, and he had also begun to
sour on New York. Originally, he had taken a three-
year lease on the apartment, he and Joan having
planned to move there permanently. Not only was it
convenient to both London and Hollywood but it was
also the home of all the important TV shows, to
which publicity-conscious Newley wanted access.
Now, however, things were different.

"I find New York ugly and oppressive," he told
colleague Arlene Francis. Newley also discovered
that he was seriously disappointed in Americans. "I
came to America with great hopes," he admitted. "I
was weaned on American pictures as a kid. I saw an
Alan Ladd movie every week." But, he said, "They
give the wrong impression. . . . The American man

[is] a weakling. He's not sure of himself. All the ads have to prove to a man that he's a man." As for the women, he complained to Francis, "The English-woman is much more attractive" and, he added tellingly, "much less domineering." (Joan kept a discreet silence, since she did not agree with his assessment of American men. She believed that it wasn't weakness but "respect" that governed their attitude toward women, and she admired how "giving" they were. But she was still too recently married, and Newley was too caught up in different emotions, to make the issue worth debating.)

How much of his attitude was due to New York and Americans, and how much was because, after a year, Hollywood hadn't come chasing after him is difficult to say. He wanted to make movies and probably couldn't accept the fact that while a Hollywood star on Broadway is a big deal, a Broadway star in Hollywood is regarded as a novice. Regardless, he wanted to get away and, since box-office receipts had fallen off dramatically—which also much have hurt his pride and colored his view of New York—he got his wish.

Where to go next, however, was a problem. Newley decided that because "the entertainment world is so spread out . . . the ideal situation would be to have a home in London and live in hotels everywhere else." However, in his tax bracket, English law would have taken up to 90 percent of his income. Thus, it was not possible to go back to England to stay until the new tax year began in April, and he refused to remain in New York. They decided to fly to Hollywood, where Newley tried to stir up some Oscar interest for *The World of Sammy Lee*, and Joan discussed some movie offers. Both efforts failed, and the couple traveled until early February, when they elected to settle down for a few months. Newley had an idea for a new play, and to give him time to work on it they took an extended lease on seventh-floor rooms at the Elysée Park Hotel in Paris. It was one of their favorite cities and the French capital was close enough to England so that they could hop over as need be to plan for their eventual relocation.

For nearly a month, Joan's days consisted of rising at nine-thirty, feeding Tara, bundling her into her perambulator, then strolling through the streets while Newley worked on *The Roar of the Greasepaint, the Smell of the Crowd*. Then, one morning, the couple were awakened by shouts from somewhere outside their suite. Going into the hall, Newley found it filled with smoke. Though the fire was centered two floors above, on the roof, he saw that both the elevator and the fire escape were inaccessible. Returning to the room, he shut the door and hurried to the balcony while Joan got the baby. She joined him on the balcony, where their shouts for help joined the more frantic cries of others above and beside them. Below, firefighters were having some difficulty connecting their hoses. Joan remembers, "It was all like a horrible nightmare, and I really thought my life was going to end." By now, smoke was everywhere inside the room. Flames were licking from the windows above them, and people were pressed against the balcony railings, shrieking for help. Finally, supported by long-overdue streams of water, firefighters were able to work their way upstairs, make a path through each corridor to the stairwell and, crawling to avoid the thick clouds of smoke, help the patrons from their rooms.

The fire was doused, and the Newleys were given another room. But Joan found herself having nightmares and insisted upon leaving not only the hotel but Paris. She suggested St. Moritz, Switzerland, where a friend of hers owned a hotel. Though Newley had no liking for the kind of phony jet-setters who frequented the ski resort, the winter crush would be over by now and he reluctantly agreed to go for the last month of their self-imposed exile.

Chapter Sixteen

*S*t. Moritz was far more pleasant for Joan than Paris. Even though Newley was not in tune with the people, he was holed up writing much of the day. Though she no longer had a nurse to help her, Joan was more content than she'd been in all her hectic, rootless years. She would take Tara down to the hotel restaurant, feeding her specially prepared food and having a great time. Often, it was just the two of them; sometimes Joan would chat with the other young mothers or, since "there was nothing else to do," go out and "spend a lot of money" on things for Tara, Newley, or herself. The only thing Joan didn't like was that almost as soon as they reached the resort, her five-month-old started waking up at six-thirty. But she was philosophical about it: vivid memories of the fire were still with her, and being up with the sun was not the worst thing that could happen.

The Newleys went back to England in April 1964, renting a house in Hampstead, near the Bricusses, where Newley and his collaborator worked round the clock on their new play—though they also managed to squeeze in the wildly popular title song for the third James Bond film, *Goldfinger*. Joan kept busy by hunting for a permanent house and shopping for clothes, but she was not entirely happy. Newley was on target when he later said, "She's a great social girl and she went and married a monk," but that was only part of it. She was getting itchy to act again. Not all of that was creative need: she also wanted the money. Unlike Joan, who was used to having and spending a lot of money—"I can't save a bob," she once confessed—her husband was newly rich. He needed to feel that his success was not fleeting before he started spending with her freedom. Joan couldn't really relate to that, but decided that rather than fight him, she'd earn her own pocket money.

The picture she was offered was *La Conguintura* which, in her words, is the story of "a woman who smuggles currency out of the country." The film was to be shot in Rome, Portofino, Lugano, and Switzerland, and while Newley wasn't thrilled about her going, especially with Tara, he knew it wasn't fair for her to be idle while he was locked up with Bricusse. Thus, in October, Joan and the year-old Tara set off for eleven hectic weeks on location.

Despite the shock of once again having early calls and long hours, not to mention the demands of her daughter, this was only the second film Joan truly loved making, *Rally 'Round the Flag, Boys!* being the first. Not only did she have a ball because *La Conguintura* was comedy, but in her judgment Vittorio Gassman—as a nobleman smuggler—was the finest actor she'd ever worked with. She also enjoyed being directed as an actress instead of as a sex object. "At Fox," she complained, "the kind of direction I got [was] 'Don't muss your hair, Joan. Turn your head, Joan, that's not your good side. Don't smile too much, Joan, you'll show your gums. More lipstick, Joan.'" Italy was a wonderful change for her.

Ultimately, the bad side about having done the film was that while it did well in Italy, *La Conguintura* barely played in England or the United States, and when it did it was under the insipid title of *One Million Dollars*. It was just Joan's luck finally to make a good movie and have it seen by fewer people than any other she had ever made.

Tara seemed to take well to the adventure, but Joan

turned down other Italian offers. She was needed: Newley and Bricusse had opened their show in the English provinces, with Norman Windom starring, and it was an unqualified failure. The flop left Newley reeling, but Broadway producer David Merrick, who'd brought *Stop the World—I Want to Get Off* to America, thought the show had potential for New York. Certainly the songs were good—among them future standards like "On a Wonderful Day Like Today" and "Who Can I Turn To?"—and the book about Cocky vs. Sir (i.e., the average person vs. the Establishment) was no worse than that of the last play. The difference, he felt, was that it didn't have Newley onstage.

To put it mildly, Newley wasn't anxious to get back into a backbreaking Broadway grind. "I wanted to act in this like I wanted to shoot myself," he said. "But Dave Merrick offers so much money you simply *can't* resist." That must have been a compelling reason, but it's also true that Newley and Bricusse had put a lot of heart into the show, and if acting in it was necessary to give it a chance, his pride left him no choice. The brilliant Cyril Ritchard was cast as Sir, and by early January 1965 the Newleys left their rented English home, sold another into which they'd intended to move, and were in New York, living in the Gotham Hotel while Joan looked for a place to live and Newley rehearsed. Then, in February, the show began a fourteen-week tour to iron out the kinks. And just to make things interesting, Joan found out she was pregnant.

The stalwart troupe—the one onstage and the mother and daughter off—played Philadelphia, Washington, New Haven, and Toronto (where, ironically, they stayed at the Elizabeth Taylor–Richard Burton Suite in the King Edward Sheraton, so named because the couple had roomed there when Burton was readying *Hamlet* for Broadway). All the while, Newley admits that he was "unbearable to live with," filled with doubt and wondering why he had jumped so quickly into writing a new show, unsure how much of his involvement was for the money and how much for self-expression. "A first show," he has said, "is like a good wine—it's been there a long time." Worrying about every facet of *The Roar of the Greasepaint, the Smell of the Crowd* both stoked his creative fires and made him question his work.

Newley praises Joan for having been "*so* sympathetic through it all," nor did she do it grudgingly: Joan was enjoying the role of supportive wife and mother. As much as she liked making movies, she admitted that "being apart is impossible"; as much as she enjoyd the glamour, she confessed, "I'm lazy" and hated "doing the things you have to do in order to promote yourself . . . that's strictly starlet time." And as much as she wanted to "settle down," tired of living out of eighty pieces of luggage, she was "too happy taking care of my baby" to regret very much at all.

Fortunately, for all the anguish and tension it caused, the show was a box-office colossus. Its tour was so successful, in fact, that it actually defrayed every penny of the production costs; by the time it hit New York in April 1965, everything was pure profit. And, like *Stop the World—I Want to Get Off*, there was a *lot* of profit. Despite a general slump on Broadway, *The Roar of the Greasepaint, the Smell of the Crowd* did so well that, after covering expenses, the backers and creators were still able to divide some $30,000 a week. Not that Newley wasn't able to find a dark lining in the silver cloud: he groused to a reporter that being back in New York "on a longterm lease . . . makes me very miserable" (to which the reporter snidely replied, "Everybody with a success on their hands should").

Instead of living in an apartment in New York, Newley decided he'd be happier renting a house in the country, and they found one in Sands Point, Long

Island. There he relaxed during the day and played with Tara, leaving for the theater late in the afternoon. Joan just vegetated. Upscale Long Island may be a wonderful place to frolic in the summer, but being pregnant, alone each evening, and not knowing a soul made it a bore for Joan. She was delighted when September came and it was necessary to move back into the city to await the birth of her second child, which she and her husband had decided they would call Caleb if a boy, Pandora if a girl.

However, a week later, on September 8, they called their newborn son Alexander Anthony Newley, though they nicknamed him Sacha so as not to be *too* mundane. Tara didn't take kindly to the new arrival and, even with a nanny, Joan had her hands full. Being in New York made things even more difficult— staying in had made her stir crazy, but going out into the busy city was hardly a balm for her nerves. Thus, Joan was not terribly upset when Hollywood came calling, even if it was Newley they wanted, and not her. The project was a screen musical adapted from Hugh Lofting's classic *Doctor Dolittle* books, with Newley being sought for the role of cat food vendor Matthew Mugg, who accompanies Dolittle on his search for the Great Pink Sea Snail. The songs, written by Bricusse, included "Talk to the Animals," which star Rex Harrison would get to sing, and Muggs's showstopping "After Today."

Newley jumped at the opportunity to make the film. *The Roar of the Greasepaint, the Smell of the Crowd* was due to close at the end of the year, which would give the Newleys plenty of time to go west and find a place to live before they moved. Newley would also have time to prerecord the songs (which he would simply mouth when acting the scene on location) before filming commenced.

For a while, Joan campaigned for the co-starring part of Emma Fairfax in the film. The character was

English, and Joan felt she would play well with Newley and Harrison. But while Fox was producing the film, Zanuck was back (he had taken control from Skouras after the debacle of *Cleopatra*) and both he and the filmmakers felt that Samatha Eggar, six years younger than Joan, would make a better Emma.

Joan was upset to lose the part. Despite having told a reporter that she "couldn't care less" if she never made another movie, she was finding that wasn't so. She was back in Hollywood, and the omnipresence of moviemaking stirred her blood. Not so coincidentally, she wasn't enjoying motherhood quite as much as she had two years before. It was a job raising two children, a job that offered very little of the kind of one-on-one joy she experienced when Tara was a baby.

With Newley's blessing, she started working again in 1966 while he was in rehearsals and sweating over his screenplay. She took a small part in a fine theatrical film called *Warning Shot*, based on the novel *711—Officer Needs Help*, which starred David Janssen as a police sergeant. Joan was twelfth-billed as the sergeant's long-suffering wife Joanie; it was on this film she first worked with Sam Wanamaker, with whom she would have considerable trouble four years later on *The Executioner*.

Joan also worked on such series as *The Man from U.N.C.L.E.*, *Mission: Impossible*, *Run for Your Life*, *The Virginian*, *The Danny Thomas Show*, *The Bob Hope Show*, and *Star Trek*—acting in what is widely considered to be *Star Trek's* finest episode, the heart-wrenching "City on the Edge of Forever." In it, star William Shatner goes back in time and falls in love with earth-woman Edith Keeler. However, she 's a pacifist and Shatner must reluctantly allow her to be run over by a car since her views would have delayed the United States from entering the Second World War and thus allowed Hitler to triumph.

During this period, Joan's marriage was not in the

best shape. The couple were living in yet another rented house, adding to the rootlessness she had grown to detest, and while he was busy with his work, she was primarily cranking out trash. Except for the one film, she was only doing television, a medium she didn't watch ("It's great for old people who can't go out," she told columnist Earl Wilson, "but I'd sooner play cards or *anything!*"), and hated on principle for the way "horrible people are always selling soap products or . . . filter tips and deodorants that last three years and magic creams that make wrinkles disappear overnight." Because each episode had to be filmed in just a few days, there was not enough time for her to do anything approaching her best work, which added to her frustration. She did it to keep busy, to make money, and to keep in the public eye.

The upshot of these various pressures was that Joan couldn't maintain the frame of mind which made her so supportive of Newley in London and New York. By the same token, he couldn't adjust to giving her the help *she* needed. As a result, they grew apart and, at times, were openly antagonistic. After three years they were experiencing what Joan refers to as "the rot," discovering, "The romantic love that we're all interested in has nothing to do with marriage." Even though she had realized, intellectually, that she must accept people, faults and all, she saw that she really didn't have the patience. Since Newley didn't either, there was nowhere for the relationship to go but down, especially in May when he broke away from the *Doctor Dolittle* rehearsals long enough to go to New York on business and Joan, alone and feeling sorry for herself, decided that the time was ripe for another of her infamous, kick-him-in-the-balls affairs.

Chapter Seventeen

For this outing, the object of her lust was twenty-five-year-old Ryan O'Neal, who was about to begin his third season as Rodney Harrington on TV's *Peyton Place*. Joan had met him at a discothèque in Beverly Hills called the Daisy, where she had gone one night hoping to lift her spirits. She danced with him that evening, but would permit the insistent young actor to go no further than driving her home. However, when O'Neal phoned on her birthday, suggesting a tête-à-tête, she joined what was to become a list of conquests second only to that of Warren Beatty: Barbra Streisand, Margaret Trudeau, Ursula Andress, Britt Ekland, Ali MacGraw, Farrah Fawcett, and many others.

At the time, O'Neal was just getting over his failed first marriage to Joanna Moore, and he was the perfect companion for Joan. She was finding that people "get on so much better" when they're not married, because they "both try harder and don't take each other for granted." Her appearance, which she'd let go to pot—"I can look like Dracula's mother, unless I'm careful"—suddenly mattered a great deal, and O'Neal was very demonstrative in showing his appreciation.

Unlike Trujillo or Stamp, O'Neal wasn't just a passing fancy with Joan. She needed a man's attention and he gave it to her, especially when the summer came and Newley finally left for England to

131

make *Doctor Dolittle.* Joan snuck over to his apartment, O'Neal came brazenly to her home, they went out together. They carried on this way for several weeks, but by then Joan's attention began to flag and her priorities came back into focus. Being away from Newley, she saw—as she confessed to one of her press representatives—that while he was unable to show love as she would like, or put work from his mind, she herself was prone to a "lack of patience and bad temper at times," and was "too quick to judge people." It wasn't exactly self-reproach, but she knew that for her own peace of mind and the sake of her family she would have to try to be a bit more tolerant of Newley. For his part, while Newley was unusually gracious about allowing other men to escort her around town, the rumors about O'Neal upset him. Still, rather than destroy the family he tried harder to be a more giving husband.

Luckily, the environment of *Doctor Dolittle* was conducive to that. The picture was being shot around Bath, in the western part of the country and one of the most beautiful spots in England. The combination of the countryside and being together in a relatively low-pressure situation improved Newley's attitude toward his wife and life in general, and gave Joan new hope that things would work out.

The Newleys passed the next eleven months in England—the eye of the storm, as it turned out. *Doctor Dolittle* finished and the family shipped itself back to Los Angeles, where Newley went right into another film, *Sweet November*, the story of a promiscuous woman (Sandy Dennis) whom Newley tries to tame. Meanwhile, with Newley's blessing, Joan and he "finally bought a house," she says, "and dedicated ourselves to furnishing it and gathering all our possessions together, as we had been traveling round like a sort of miniature circus for so long." So good a job did Joan do putting together *her* house that she was commissioned to redecorate the homes of several associates, and spent a few weeks doing little more than "going round getting curtain and sofa samples," which she found refreshingly different.

From August to November, Joan barely saw her husband. Universal was interested in the autobiographical film he'd been writing, *Can Hieronymus Merkin Ever Forget Mercy Humppe and Find True Happiness?*, and he spent the time polishing the script in the hopes of getting it filmed.

Joan did more television, most notably playing a villain on the popular *Batman* series: Lorelei Circe (aka the Siren) who debilitated her adversaries with a remarkable seven-octave voice. Star Adam West recalls Joan as being "very sweet and extremely cooperative, a pleasure to be around," though he says that for some reason "the director made things terrible for her, and she became very sad, very frustrated and intimidated. I didn't like that and tried to make her comfortable, but he *really* gave her a rough time, bringing her almost to tears." Thinking about it later, West says he realized that Joan was probably a target because so many people in the business "misunderstood" her, widely perceiving Joan as an undisciplined hedonist and a discredit to the acting craft. He, however, saw nothing of the sort, finding her "not at all frivolous or angry or throwing any kind of a tantrum." His assessment is echoed by other actors with whom she worked during this period, suggesting that despite the comedown of having to do TV after being on the silver screen, Joan was genuinely glad to have the work.

Although both Joan and Newley had their hands full with sundry projects, they made time in August to become the co-founders of a new discothèque in West Hollywood. Called the Factory, it was established in response to widespread disappointment in the Daisy—poor food, undisciplined crowds, and taped music were among the commonly voiced complaints. Together with Paul Newman, Sammy Davis, Jr., Pierre Salinger, Peter Lawford, and others, the Newleys bought an old, two-story factory, refurbished the inside in what the *New York Times* described as "turn-of-the-century bawdy-house-elegant style," with a large bar, fifty tables and booths, and a large dance floor with bandstand. Dues were set at $500, and Newley appointed himself director of press relations—his job beginning and ending when he banished all members of the press in order to maintain the privacy which its members cherished.

For a while, the Factory "caught on beyond our wildest expectations," says Joan, and "was a tremendously stimulating experience." However, like so many things in fickle Hollywood, it faded after a few months, and the illustrious directors were forced to abandon it. By that time, however, the Newleys were out of the country again. At the end of 1967, literally on the spur of the moment, Newley decided to go to London so he could spend a few weeks with Herbert Kretzmer, his collaborator on the songs for *Hieronymus Merkin*. Thus, with three days to prepare, the family was once again bundled off to England, this time staying in Jackie's Hampstead apartment. Having just remarried—her first husband had died—Jackie had moved out, taking all her furniture with her, and Joan complains, "I had to rush around hiring beds, cots, tables, chairs, etc., and more or less camping in the flat until we rented a large maisonette in Mayfair." That came only after six cramped weeks, when Universal finally had the completed script and songs in hand and gave Newley the go-ahead to make his directorial debut.

Can Hieronymus Merkin Ever Forget Mercy Humppe and Find True Happiness? is a film of remarkable invention, if somewhat unconventional structure and often obscure symbolism. Nevertheless, the word "autobiographical" was used to describe it.

The narrative is framed by a beach party at which former stage star and singer Merkin screens a film about his life. Among those on hand are his two young children Thumbelina and Thaxted, his wife Polyester Poontang—who did not take the name of Merkin when she married—and a trio of critics who serve as a Greek chorus about the film/life they are seeing. The film unreeled by Merkin ranges from straight narrative to surrealism as he tries (and fails) to avoid involvement with a succession of girls, of whom Mercy Humppe is at once the most tempting and elusive; as well as having to deal with his colleague Good Time Eddie Filth and white-suited Fate. In the end, Merkin is left poised on a mountaintop, dressed in a white gown, his arms outstretched like a modern-day Jesus—Newley's view of life being that it's ultimately a paradox: we're martyred for the good we do, and crucified for the bad.

The supporting roles were all well cast. Milton Berle was tapped as Mr. Filth, George Jessel was hired to play Fate with a ready supply of one-liners (years before George Burns played God), and *Playboy* centerfold Connie Kreski undraped again to star as Mercy Humppe. Less inspired, but far more appropriate, was the casting of Newley, Tara, Sacha, and Joan as the Merkins.

Newley had cast the children early on, feeling that, though they were young, it might help them to understand *him* better if they got a firsthand taste of the kind of work he did. Yet Joan had not been slated to play the part of Polyester Poontang. "Tony didn't write the part for me," she says, "and had no intention of casting me in it until he had suggested other people and Herman Raucher pointed out that I was the only actress exactly right for the part." Newley obviously felt that having her in the film would hit too close to home, since she would already be on location looking after the children when they weren't working. When Joan was finally invited aboard, it was clearly as much for financial as creative reasons, helping to keep the budget down by taking some $5,000—far less than a disinterested third party would have required.

Since there was some time before her scenes would have to be shot, Joan accepted a low-budget spy film called *Subterfuge*, quite possibly the worst film of its type every made. Gene Barry stars as an American agent and Joan plays the wife of a different agent who turns out to be a turncoat. Joan did a good job, but her performance was the only good one in this dull, predictable film.

Subterfuge was filmed during January and February, after which Newley's film began its four-month shoot in London and in very Catholic Malta, where there were some extremely vocal denunciations of the project from shocked locals. Years later, when she didn't like Newley anymore, Joan would go quite a distance out of her way to badmouth the effort; at the time, however, she was one of its biggest supporters. She said of Polyester that the role was "more enjoyable than anything else I've ever played . . . I understand this character," and of the film itself, "It's full of the subtle tongue-in-cheek humor I adore [and] I think it's definitely the best film I've ever been in. It has so many different levels, all of which can be enjoyed by the people acting in it and the same goes for viewing it. Everyone can derive what they like out of it." Joan also said that she found Newley a stimulating director and wanted to work with him again because "he has a wonderful rapport with the actors and actresses."

The Newleys stayed on in London through the rest of 1967 and most of 1968, while he edited the film and supervised the postproduction work. For the most part, the year was a satisfying one. Not that Joan was surprised: her horoscope had predicted that 1968 would be good for her, and by this time she was so entranced with astrology that it had replaced psychiatry in her life. She told the *Daily Express* at the time,

"I'm a great believer in it. I had this astrologer in Beverly Hills [Ben Gary], who predicted his own death and Warren's career, exactly. He also predicted my marriage and how many children I'd have." But Gary had likewise seen her divorcing Newley after seven years, and in the back of her mind that thought haunted Joan. Thus, she was not surprised that after his surge of attentiveness, Newley was once more distant and self-absorbed. However, Joan felt that more than the movie was preoccupying him—specifically, she suspected Connie Kreski, among other young ladies Newley had met on the film. Regardless of how much of this hunch was based on lipstick stains and how much on innate suspicion ("I trust my choice of men all right," she told columnist Roderick Mann, "it's just that I don't trust men"), Joan convinced herself that she was perfectly justified in having yet another fling of her own.

This time the object of her wandering eye was thirty-three-year-old Ron Kass, an M.I.T. graduate, a jazz trombonist, and an executive with the Beatles' record company, Apple. He'd been invited to dine with the Newleys by a mutual friend, and before long, while Newley worked and went his own way, Kass and Joan were dining alone—among other things. She was totally smitten by him: tall, tanned, outgoing, and showing as much interest in Joan's mind as in her body. He managed to balance good living with hard work, keeping a splendid humor all the while. And he had nothing of Newley's temperament—or genius—which, just then, was exactly what Joan wanted.

The marriage to Newley was on the way out, though Newley obviously didn't know it had even been in danger. While they were shooting *Can Hieronymus Merkin Ever Forget Mercy Humppe and Find True Happiness?*, he had been sitting in bed with her and came across an article in a movie magazine which announced that they were going to split. Newley recalls, "I said, 'Why do you keep these things from me? A wife who is planning to walk out . . . should let her husband know.' Oh well," he concluded, "I guess these things are part of the game."

With Joan, however, moving from man to man was no game—as her new Mr. Wonderful would soon learn.

Chapter Eighteen

Joan was even less secretive about Kass than she'd been about O'Neal and it wasn't long before Newley noticed that something was going on. Since there was nothing he could do about it, nor she about his priorities, they decided to come to terms. Though the two of them would continue to live together for the children's well-being, they would separate. Returning to Los Angeles, they were able to maintain the charade until the combination of personal and professional disappointments finished the union for good.

The beginning of the end came when Newley's cinematic labor of love was a commercial disaster. Although its sexual content was widely plugged in *Playboy*, which should have helped at the box office, the movie was the sixth to be hamstrung with an "X" rating, therefore limiting the markets in which it could play. Worse, the film was widely panned, not just because it was flawed but because it had the audacity to aspire to the psychoanalytical abstractions which only Fellini was permitted to make.

Needless to say, the first-time director was profoundly discouraged. *Doctor Dolittle* had also been a failure, and he feared for the future of his screen career; as it turned out he had every right to, since he has yet to make his mark in film. Years later, Joan would remark, "There's something rather sad and bitter about Tony today because he hasn't made it as big as he would have liked." He remains, however, a popular figure on the lucrative tour circuit, an in-demand lyricist, and an extraordinary talent.

Despite her comments, Joan didn't fare much better in 1969. In addition to having done the Newley picture, three other pictures were considerably less than rewarding: *If It's Tuesday, This Must Be Belgium* was a modest hit, but her part was a cameo; the Italian *State of Siege*—no relation to the 1973 Costa-Gavras triumph—was an amateurish film in which Joan was a widow who fell for a teenager; and *Drive Hard, Drive Fast*, a TV movie. That one, made in Los Angeles at year's end, was the story of a race car driver (Brian Kelly) who, thanks to the machinations of evil Collins, becomes involved with murder. The film was so bad that Universal watched it sit on the shelf for nearly four years before it was finally aired.

However, at least Joan had come out of the year with a lover, so all was right with the world. Newley wasn't so lucky.

The couple separated physically in October 1969 and filed for divorce in January. It was granted the following August, Newley being ordered to pay $1,250 a month in child support. However, over the next few years he would bring himself to the brink of disaster by "letting millions slip through my hands," and in 1981 Joan would finally haul him into court claiming he was derelict by some $40,000 in support payments. It took Newley two years, but with the support of his wife, Dareth, a former stewardess, he got back on his feet financially.

Anyone familiar with Joan Collins's career, and

who read her comments to the press about Newley's bitterness, would have wondered what high horse she'd climbed off. If anything, her own career was even less spectacular than his and, as though aware of her own apparent hypocrisy, Joan made a point of remarking in interviews that she had no interest in stardom. Her goal in life, she said, was "to enjoy every minute I can with my family." Acting was something she did to earn money and because she enjoyed it, but that was as far as her ambition went. Besides, said Joan—taking a contrived swipe at the successes—"Even some of the superstars go to pieces, for it's just as hard to remain at the top as it is to get there."

Despite such pronouncements, Joan was not without her regrets. Where would she be had she concentrated on her career rather than panting after Warren Beatty and then becoming wife to Newley and mother to his children? (Wrote reporter Roderick Mann, "So much time has Miss Collins devoted to love, [and] the pursuit thereof, that it has always baffled me how she found time to make any films at all.") Even if it were not stardom she wanted, Joan certainly yearned to be respected as an actress— something that had eluded her in almost every part she'd undertaken since her earliest films at Rank. And the problem was more acute now that she was getting old: at thirty-seven, Joan was over the hill by Hollywood standards.

"I tried to get back into movies," she said, but "there was no such animal as a leading lady over thirty." The result: "A long period of feeling really washed-up," of knowing what she wanted, yet looking down the road and seeing nothing but TV movies and second-rate action pictures. Charles Schneer, the producer of one of her next films, capsulized it quite well when he said that he felt she "deeply resented not being able to score in the dramatic field," resentment heightened because she had spent so much of her time in London, "living among the giants."

Since she was still flush with the glow of seeing Ron Kass, Joan was able to shrug off her professional disappointments. "At the moment," she told journalist Clive Hirschhorn, "my career is a very secondary thing compared to my private life." But that would fade. Despite her stiff upper lip, she got tired of going to the studio to do a low-budget film or TV show, of "turning up at the gate, saying my name was Joan Collins, and always getting the same answer: 'Joan who?' You can only take just so much of that."

She kept up her spirits by getting a JOANWHO license plate, and reinforced her worth by trashing Hollywood to the press. She said snidely that while Hollywood prided itself on being farsighted, it was way behind Miss Joan Collins and London. She said, "It takes about two years for a fashion to reach here—just when it's finished over there. I remember when I wore a miniskirt in Beverly Hills two years ago being glared at angrily by an irate group of blue-rinsed matrons in mink stoles and flowered hats. They hated me." For all its bluster, she said that Hollywood had a "love of conformity," as if to imply that that was the *real* reason they didn't like her, Joan being anything but a conformist. Later, she tried to make not being in the front ranks seem like a virtue. "I don't want to kick America," she said before going ahead and kicking it, "but nowadays there is something tatty and shoddy about the way they are doing things in Hollywood." Specifically, she observed, "I seem to have cornered the American television market for playing hookers. I suppose I have the appearance of having been around without looking used." Regardless of her personal disappointments, she pointed out—truthfully, as it happens— "At the moment, so many of the best films are not being made in Hollywood."

Naturally, with all the formulaic TV and grade-B

movies, the only thing for an artist of her aspirations to do was to leave, which she did. As soon as the divorce papers were filed, Joan made plans to return with the children to England, granting Newley the freedom to see them whenever he wished. Swallowing her pride, she did one more film before leaving, *Three in the Cellar*, about a young man whose claim to fame is his sexual prowess. As it happened, after all her beefing, this film turned out to be the nadir of her most recent stay in Tinseltown. Elsewhere in the industry, Ryan O'Neal was shooting *Love Story*, Glenda Jackson—a RADA alumnus three years her junior who had gone onto the stage—was acting in *Women in Love*, which would win her an Oscar, Natalie Wood had just had a mammoth hit with *Bob & Carol & Ted & Alice*, and youngsters Jane Fonda, Genevieve Bujold, and Liza Minnelli were the talk of the town. Joan, meanwhile, was acting in a third-rate film with another over-the-hill actor, Larry Hagman. Regardless of the disclaimers she made, that must have hurt.

Back in England, her beloved homeland, things actually got worse. Faced with the kind of career crisis Joan was experiencing, most actors give up the profession and become screenwriters, directors, producers, or real estate brokers. Since she was not a quitter and had to earn a living, she intended to put up with everything the business threw at her. But with a slight change.

Says one of her producers from the early seventies, Joan was possessed with a new need, and "was constantly fighting to stay young." While that is a natural enough pursuit for most actresses, Joan would approach the façade-making with the same kind of I'll-show-'em attitude that had marked her departure from RADA, a corollary of her old philosophy, expressed to Earl Wilson back in 1957: "If somebody tells me many times to do a certain thing, I don't do it." If industryites kept hinting to Joan that she was too old and getting older, she'd show *them*. Like Dorian Gray, she'd get *younger*. It wasn't so bad in 1970, but so compulsive would this behavior become that, a few years later, a photographer was warned by a publicist before shooting her, "Don't say you met her ten years ago. Say 'several.' Several is nicer." So annoyed did British journalist Neil Lyndon become that he wrote: "Miss Collins does not count the years according to the convention that two and two make four: she has her own system, as puzzling as Chinese writing. All temporal truths pass through the scrambler of her historical view."

Joan, of course, had what she felt was a perfectly good reason for fudging her age. "When it comes to casting," she said, "hanging an age on someone is like hanging a label around their neck as far as producers and directors are concerned. One should be allowed to be the age one looks rather than the age it says on your birth certificate." She also thought, "It's rather rude." But that was a feint, since everyone in the business more or less knew how old she was. She was trying to sell the public the idea that while Joan Collins "may seem to have been around forever," she was still a spring chicken.

Though they were constant companions, Joan and Kass lived apart. Her tastes were as expensive as ever and, without Newley to support her—and with Kass having to pay for the upkeep of his three sons from a previous marriage—Joan went on a work binge.

The first picture on her slate was *The Executioner*. Filmed in London and Greece, it was directed by Sam Wanamaker, with whom she had worked on *Warning Shot*. Her work in the film lasted only three or four weeks, but they were weeks the director would remember. Producer Schneer says, "Sam is a very good actor's director, because he *is* an actor. He knows how they like to be treated." But Joan was in no frame of mind to take direction from Sam or anyone else. In addition to the offensive aftertaste of Hollywood, and feeling trapped in another film which she more or less had to do to pay the rent, she was involved with Kass. He stayed with Joan at her hotel in Athens, and the two of them spent a lot of time fighting.

Kass was then in a state of professional upheaval, having left Apple to take a position with a different company, which he would soon leave for yet another. His patience could not have been at its peak, and though he was quick to encourage and support Joan, he was equally quick to speak out when he thought she was wrong. Joan, of course, was no less forthright in responding, which often soured her temper on the set in much the same way that personal problems had taken their toll on *Decameron Nights* years before. Then, when they would make up, she would want to be with Kass regardless of the demands of the film—just as she had run to Warren Beatty during *Esther and the King*.

Joan doesn't deny that she had changed. "Marriage," she says, "tends to make you more selfish [and] the more you marry, the more selfish you become." She had spent so much time catering to men that she fully intended to cater to herself. "For a long time I'd be whatever a man wanted me to be. It was a throwback to wanting to please Daddy as a little girl. Now I've got sufficient respect for my opinions to say, 'Look, this is the way I am and if you don't like it, well, I'm sorry.'"

Wanamaker tried to keep her attention on the project, but it was often a lost cause, especially when it came time for Joan to appear seminude in one scene. She exhibited what Schneer calls "mock modesty" since she had done a similar scene in *State of Siege*, but Joan was adamant about showing skin in her native land where, among other things, she was no doubt concerned that her children might see the film. "I won't ever strip in a movie," she told one journalist. "It's not that I'm old-fashioned and a stick-in-the-mud, it's just that I think a woman (or a man, for that matter) is more exciting with her clothes on. Garbo never stripped. Dietrich kept her clothes on, and so did Vivien Leigh. And who is more glamourous than them?" Although she failed to realize that they belonged to a different generation and were bona fide stars, she concluded on more solid ground, "I honestly believe that actresses have a certain responsibility to their audiences—a responsibility never to offend them."

Yet *The Executioner*, for all its failings, was at least a mainstream film, a picture that had some appeal to all audiences. For the next few years, Joan would make only low-budget science-fiction and horror films. And if she was unhappy being a little fish in a big pond, she found that being a big fish in a little pond was actually a demotion.

Chapter Nineteen

After The Executioner, Joan realized that her approach to life and work was not quite what it should be. For whatever reason, no one was going to offer her great parts—maybe not ever. It didn't matter whether she'd been away too long, was too old, had become too closely identified with sex-symbol parts, or—her personal theory— "because one has enjoyed one's life, people think you can't be serious when you do work." She was not in demand, and unless she cooperated the alternative was to slit her wrists or to starve because bitterness drove her to disruptive antics which made her persona non grata. Since these were not viable options, she knew that she would have to accept whatever work was around, and behave professionally on any film she undertook. Given the caliber of many of these, that was a tall order.

To help her through the dark days, Joan attended a seminar in Actualization, "which," she says, "is a bit like the better-known est. You are locked in from Thursday afternoon until Sunday. You come out aware of yourself, more positive." That helped her find things to like in herself even when she was doing things which strained her self-respect.

Throughout the dim days of her career which followed, Joan also derived a great deal of strength and joy from Kass and her family. Tara, now seventeen, had been dating for two years and Joan fretted, ached, and soared with her. "I would hate it if they were promiscuous," she said of her children. "I don't think that makes for a good life." But she was glad when her daughter had a boyfriend, since "I want my children to be with someone who makes them happy . . . I love them more than anyone else in my life."

Joan loved Kass, though at this point she was as unlikely a candidate for the altar as she'd ever been. "I am very skeptical about marriage now. Who wouldn't be—a two-time loser? I have a real fear of going through it again." Joan's concerns were not only for herself but for the children: she didn't want them going through the emotional wringer of getting and then possibly losing a "new daddy."

But having two separate residences in London was expensive, and after two years they decided to find a house and make a home.

In the meantime, Joan found herself suddenly in

demand. A horror craze had swept the world beginning in 1957, when the popularity of old monster movies on TV inspired Hammer Productions of England to make *The Curse of Frankenstein*, the first color monster movie and one of the most graphic. Stars Christopher Lee and Peter Cushing became box-office titans, and Hammer followed it with a slew of films about vampires, werewolves, mummies, witches, zombies, mythical beasts, and other such fiends.

Except for the horror films, the British film industry was in a depressed state. The old days were gone, Ealing was no more, and anyone who wanted to work swallowed his pride and acted with—or sometimes *as*—a bloody ghoul or an aggressive alien. Yet what was amazing about these films was how they transformed has-beens into superstars. Joan's Fox colleague, Barbara Steele, had gone to Italy to make horror films and returned a conquering queen; by acting in *The Curse of Frankenstein*, forty-one-year-old Hazel Court revitalized *her* fading British film career. It wasn't exactly prestigious work, but it was steady and quick.

In 1971 Joan did a trio of films of these bizarre, low-budget pictures: *Quest For Love*, a silly romance about a man who travels from our world to an earthlike dimension; the improbably titled *Inn of the Frightened People*, the story of parents who go on a murderous spree to avenge the killing of their daughter; and *Fear in the Night*, in which a woman is stalked through the corridors of a boys' school.

Joan didn't aspire to Steele-like notoriety. If her performances are any indication, she more or less walked through these films, scanning the horizon for more promising projects. She didn't need a *Cleopatra*; a script with just a little meat would have been sufficient. Occasionally, a project of this type came along. On television she had fun guest-starring on series like *The Persuaders*, with Roger Moore and Tony

Curtis, and *Great Mysteries*, which was hosted by Orson Welles. More challenging for her were *The Man Who Came to Dinner* for the *Hallmark Hall of Fame* and *Fallen Angels*, though the former did not live up to her expectations. She said that the two-hour special, which aired on NBC in the U.S., "was a dreadful experience." Although the part of Lorraine Sheldon was a fulfilling one, Joan claims that Orson Welles "treat[ed] most of the people on the set very badly," and managed to spoil the project for her. (Objectively speaking, Welles was ideally cast as Sheridan Whiteside, the man who meddles in the affairs of his host family; it is not inconceivable that Welles's bad behavior was, in fact, just his puckish way of putting the cast in an appropriately uncomfortable frame of mind.) The second play, by Noel Coward, starred Joan and Susannah York as lifelong friends who are in love with the same man. Though *Fallen Angels* aired only in England, Joan enjoyed working with York and found it a rewarding experience.

But when these were over, it was back to the horror films. Luckily, there was a good one in the pack.

Back in 1946, Basil Dearden and three other directors had teamed to make *Dead of Night*, a film made up of several short stories. Founding Amicus Productions with his partner Max Rosenberg, horror aficionado Milton Subotsky revived the anthology form and gave new life to the fading horror field.

The most successful picture Subotsky made was based on a popular comic book from the 1950s, *Tales from the Crypt*. This 1972 film was not only the most popular of Joan's pictures from this era, it was far and away the best. Joan's episode was a classic chiller. She starred as Joanne, a woman who becomes so fed up with her husband's mediocrity that she decides to kill him.

One of the things that made *Tales from the Crypt* palatable to Joan was the caliber of the cast. Subotsky knew that top-name stars lent dignity and talent to the genre, and was willing to spend the money to get Joan, Ralph Richardson, Nigel Patrick, Richard Greene, and the by then much-in-demand Peter Cushing, among others. He paid Joan some £10,000 for a week's work.

In contrast to her work habits on other films, Subotsky reports that Joan "was very cooperative. She stayed overtime and was no problem at all." Director Freddie Francis, who, ironically, as a cinematographer had won an Oscar for *Sons and Lovers*, agrees. "She was very, very professional and very good." He also noted that although she wasn't a star, she carried herself like one. "She's that type who, when she comes on the set and gets in front of the camera, that's *her* camera. It isn't a selfishness: if you offer your services as a film star, you *should* project yourself right into that camera. Unfortunately," he adds, "it has to be to hell with the other guy." Something at which, by then, the increasingly territorial Joan was becoming very good.

Joan enjoyed making the film, though it did require six takes for her to hit her husband with the brass poker *just so*. Neither Francis nor Subotsky will speculate on whether she enjoyed having a proxy mate at her mercy, though she was heard to quip, "It's getting more and more difficult to murder your husband these days."

For all the comparative quality of this film, and for all of her professionalism on the set, Joan was openly hostile to the genre. During the making of the film, she said she was tired of the blood and graphic nature of horror pictures. "It makes me sick," she said succinctly. "As an actress and a mother, I feel things are going much too far in the area of violence." Yet she continued to make them: *Tales from the Crypt* was followed in 1973 by *Tales that Witness Madness*, another omnibus film from Subotsky, and in 1974 by *Dark Places*, about a young man who is possessed by the spirit of a mad killer.

Before she made those two films, however, the thirty-nine-year-old actress took time out to have another baby.

Joan has never said whether Katyana Kennedy Kass, born June 20, 1972, was a surprise; suffice it to say that she and Kass had married that same year. The baby joined the couple and Joan's two children in a house Joan had found earlier. The three-story home was located on Sheldon Avenue in Highgate, a peaceful, upper-class suburb north of Central London. Joan had fallen in love with the place on sight. "It's a solid, family sort of house," she said. "To me, it combines the best elements of country and city life. We have a flower garden, pure air, and are only twenty minutes from London."

One of the pastimes that kept up Joan's spirits during her horror "slump" was decorating the six-bedroom, red-brick Tudor house. Silver wallpaper in the living room, a marble tub and antiques for the bathroom, a screening room on the top floor, and original art by Dali and Miro on the walls. It was as eclectic and unpredictable as Joan, and she loved it. It wasn't the first house she'd owned, but it was the first place she really felt was a home. And if pictures like *Inn of the Frightened People* were necessary to keep up the payments, then that was how it would have to be.

Joan also kept active—and young—by exercising. "When I was expecting Katy," she says, "I went to a Harley Street doctor and asked if there were any special precautions I should take to ensure that I would get my figure back afterward." She adds sagely, "The third one is the critical one, you know. Women can usually keep their figure for two children, but after the third they hardly ever do." The doctor told her there was nothing she could do, so Joan went to a doctor in New York. "He told me that I must on no account put on more than seventeen pounds in the pregnancy, and I should exercise."

Finding a gym in Ladbroke Road in London, she went there twice a week. She kept going even after Katy was born, noting in her own inimitable way, "[Men] think they are taking exercise with the odd round of golf. Then they take a mistress, overdo it, have a heart attack. I want to live to be an active old lady." Her desire for youth was heightened even more as she watched the children grow. Though she was "totally committed" to them, their maturation underscored the fact that "the time will come when they leave me." The last thing she wanted was to be a "poor old mum whining about how I've devoted my life to them"; she wanted to be just like a friend in California who "looks about fifty-four but is over seventy." So Joan, the nonsportive girl who never did anything more active than play charades, exercised.

In spite of the dearth of good parts, Joan was not entirely resigned to spending her life as a "gore girl." In 1973, Kass got his feet wet as a moviemaker by co-producing a film for Joan's friend Peter Sellers, and it was he who produced Joan's *Fallen Angels*. By 1974 he was feeling confident enough to go into it full-time. He received further encouragement from his friend Edgar Bronfman, a multimillionaire who had dabbled in film and was interested in getting into it on a regular basis. Joan liked being with Bronfman, too, in part because they flitted around the world on his private jet. Bronfman, in his forties, had the kind of young lifestyle which appealed to her, and while she was in London Joan exclaimed, "I'm enjoying myself more than I ever did in my twenties. I even feel more attractive!"

Just like Dorian Gray.

When she wasn't jet-setting and decorating, Joan made a slew of films which ranged from fair to abysmal. An Italian film, *L'Arbitro* (*The Referee*), and the Spanish *Call of the Wolf* (*The Great Adventure* in the U.S.) were stultifying, but a trio of British films, while

cheaply made, were not without redeeming qualities.
Alfie Darling (*Oh! Alfie!* in the U.S.), made in 1974 and
based on a novel by Bill Naughton, featured an
engaging performance by Alan Price as Alfred Elkins,
"a randy sod" who lives to seduce women until he
falls in love with magazine editor Abigail Summers
(Jill Townsend). Joan, however, is only briefly seen as
an adulterous nymphomaniac named Fay, who has to
utter such deathless prose as, "Oh, you dirty, rotten
swine" when she's in the heat of passion. Curiously,
despite her complaints on *The Executioner*, Joan
elected to bare her chest for the cameras in this film.
The fact that the camera did not dwell on her and the
whole thing was erotic rather than clinically porno-
graphic no doubt helped overcome her resistance.
Perhaps her father said it best when he told the *Daily
Star*, "It doesn't matter that she has to strip off in
some of the parts. She looks good and that's what
goes these days."

Joan was better served by another pair of films she
made during 1975. She was witty and vivacious as
Black Bess, a highwaywoman in *The Bawdy Adventures
of Tom Jones*, based on the London stage play, and
suitably terror-stricken as a cursed woman in the
popular horror film *I Don't Want to Be Born* (*The Devil
Within Her* in the U.S.). She also managed to land a
guest spot on the new syndicated series *Space: 1999*,
playing Kara, spokeswoman for a race of cannibalistic
aliens. It wasn't a great role, but the new show was a
huge hit worldwide and gave her that priceless
commodity all actors crave: exposure.

Joan was now making two or three films a year; and
was actually getting better quality scripts when her
world underwent one of its annoyingly predictable
upheavals. A new tax structure was adopted in
England, making it impossible for Joan and Ron to
own all their material things, remain in England, and
stay solvent. With greater reluctance than when she
had left England with Newley years before, in June

1975 Joan and her family were once again forced to relocate. And if it wasn't bad enough to be leaving a home she loved and a career showing the stirrings of rebirth, she was going back to loathsome California so that Kass could produce and she could act.

As it turned out, most of Joan's best acting was offscreen. For the sake of her family, she had to pretend she was happy when she couldn't have been more miserable.

Chapter Twenty

"*I* loathe television. I hate to watch it."

Joan was still talking down TV to the press, though when she relocated back in Southern California, that was just about all anyone was offering her.

The Kass–Newley–Collins conglomeration moved into a sprawling house on Chalette Drive, a wide, airy, ritzy street located just north of Beverly Hills proper, in Trousdale Estates. Financially, they were in over their heads and Joan knew it, though she optimistically hoped that things would work out. Not long after they were settled in, an astrologer predicted that Joan would have "the possibility of enormous fame if I took an opportunity that would be presented to me . . . in America." Though the prediction was typically vague astrological bunkum, Joan was encouraged—falsely, as it turned out.

For a year after the move, Joan did nothing but television. She went to Hawaii for *Starsky and Hutch*, reteamed with Robert Wagner on *Switch*, and did any other series which came calling. The most prestigious of her efforts during this time was the sixth-billed part of Avril Devereaux in the Paramount miniseries based on Arthur Hailey's *The Moneychangers*. Aired in four parts on NBC's *Big Event* in December 1976, the six-and-one-half-hour saga was about a pair of banking executives (Kirk Douglas and Christopher Plummer) who become engaged in a power struggle. Unfortunately, the part did little for Joan. Most of the publicity went to actress Jean Peters, who had come out of retirement after years of being Mrs. Howard Hughes, and while the program won a slew of Emmys, including Plummer as best actor, Joan's exceptional work as the call girl went unrecognized.

By the summer of 1976, Joan had sunk to her worst frame of mind since returning to the U.S. Not only was her own career rolling along in neutral, with Joan collecting only a few thousand dollars per show and numerous rejections—"One casting director told me I'd never play a mother," says Joan wryly—but Kass's attempts to become a producer suddenly and unexpectedly stalled. The year before, Edgar Bronfman had set up Sagittarius Productions, with Kass as its head. However, the eccentric Bronfman inexplicably soured on the film business and dissolved Sagittarius, leaving Kass unemployed.

Joan went back to Actualizations to help keep her sanity, sold their expensive home for a cheaper one, and even collected unemployment while Kass tried to put together film projects for Joan, for himself or, actually, for anyone. He went to meetings, saw film executives, pitched ideas, and failed to bring in a cent. Discouraged, he started putting on weight; soon, he would be turning to more than food for comfort.

For her part, Joan threw herself into an exercise program which dwarfed what she'd done back in London. Keeping physically active and thinking young was the best way for her to discourage depression, and she did it with a fitness guru named Kim Lee, who had a studio in West Hollywood called Kinetic Integral Movement (KIM). "Here in California, there's a whole body cult," she told *Women's Wear Daily* in September 1976, "and now I'm turned off by people who don't take care of themselves." KIM was the place to take care of oneself, she insisted, and became something of the studio's unofficial spokesperson. Lee appreciated the publicity—and so did Joan.

As fall drew to a close, Joan accepted a film called *Empire of the Ants*, a science-fiction thriller which was a follow-up to the hugely successful *Food of the Gods*. The initial film was inspired by the H. G. Wells novel *Food of the Gods*, in which an unknown substance causes animals to grow to giant size. In the sequel, radioactive waste was responsible for creating a colony of giant ants on an isolated island.

Both films were the work of director Bert I. Gordon, one of the most successful producers of low-budget science-fiction pictures. The films were being backed by American International, which had a knack for making huge hits out of inexpensive but well-cast fantasy pictures. Fifteen years before, the studio had revitalized the career of Vincent Price by sticking him into cheap but superbly crafted adaptations of the works of Edgar Allan Poe. Joan didn't like the idea of doing another horror picture—acting in them had done little more than help her "get good at screaming," forgetting the money she made with them—but she needed the cash, and there was always the chance that this film would give her career a Price-like boost.

The soft-spoken, forty-four-year-old Gordon has always been fond of making movies on location. "You get more in a film," he maintains, "not only visually, but in the performances." So, in November he took cast members Collins, Robert Lansing, Robert Pine,

Albert Salmi, John David Carson, and Jacqueline Scott, along with a small crew, to Florida, to a town called Belle Glade near Lake Okeechobee. He also brought along the several giant wire-and-rubber ants which would be operated off camera by special effects technicians.

Not long after they arrived in Florida, location-lover Gordon found himself at odds with his cast. They were shooting in the marshlands of the Everglades where conditions were not as pristine as in a studio. Robert Lansing recalls, "My favorite story is about this scene where Joanie starts to run away from the group, then she sees a giant ant for the first time. She runs back into my arms and we have a little scene where I tell her to take it easy. I say, 'Let's get out of here,' but all of a sudden neither of us could move. We'd gone down into the swamp, stuck, sinking as we spoke."

Lansing didn't like the location, and he wasn't alone. Although he says, "Joanie was great, like a good girl on a picnic, she *detested* the swamp, not only because it was remote but because she happens to be terribly afraid of snakes." ("I think it has something to do with—uh, you *know*," she once told Johnny Carson, alluding to the male sexual organ.) Lansing remembers, "You didn't know where they were—or the alligators and the crocodiles. And since it was a small crew, you didn't have the kind of security you'd have on a big crew with everyone beating the bush."

The director denies that the stars were ever in any danger, despite claims to the contrary by Lansing and by Joan, who spends several pages criticizing Gordon in her autobiography, *Past Imperfect*. "It *was* the roughest jungle we could find; it *had* live crocodiles." But, he says, the carnivores were driven far back by a barrage of blanks before the actors went near the water, and he had the cooperation of the state of Florida as well as animal experts in preparing the site for filming. "In all my films I'm very careful," he insists. "There isn't much left to chance."

While the site was undoubtedly uncomfortable at times, it is clear that what was really bugging some of the actors was not just the possibility that a snake might slither by. Rather, they seemed to be annoyed because they were away from home during the holiday season, and were making a film they didn't really want to make. Then, too, they resented the time Gordon had to spend on the special effects. "He was a bit of a *putz*, a pain in the ass," says Lansing. "He was so involved with giant ants that he didn't [give] all his energies to the story and actors." The actors dealt with Gordon by banding together—the "artists" against the heartless producer, as it were. But that was more or less a symbolic gesture. "You're there," says Lansing, "so what can you do? Leave? You give it your best shot and yell a lot."

Gordon, however, does not feel he was unfair to anyone; he is, in fact, a man of great integrity, utterly lacking in pretention. Without directly naming Joan or any other actress, he says, "Some people resent the fact that they have to do something for money. Well, that's *their* problem. If a prostitute is on the street and she's doing it because she has to do it, I feel sorry for her but that's her problem. If an actress *deals* with her problem by lashing out in print, then she shouldn't take the job. Everyone who works in a film meets the director ahead of time, and knows the location." Gordon insists that nothing on the film was a surprise, and not only feels it is unprofessional for actors who are paid "damn well" to "get their hostilities out [by] badmouthing a film," but that any director—again, naming no names—"could possibly double something in spades if he were so inclined."

Escaping from Florida in the closing days of December, Joan agreed to go to Chicago a few weeks later to act in the play *Murder Among Friends* at the Pheasant Run Playhouse. Local theaters paid several thousand dollars a week to have has-been actresses appear for a few weeks; good wages for the work. However, Joan bowed out at the last minute, telling the theater operators that she was "physically exhausted." They were stunned and furious. "She left us high and dry," said a spokesperson, "and we're contemplating legal action." However, Joan's manager, Tom Korman, said righteously, "Joan had just finished *Empire of the Ants* in the Florida Everglades, and simply was knocked out. She was sick." It was, however, apparently a smokescreen, since Joan was photographed dancing with Kass in a New York night spot while she was supposed to be knocked out and sick. The affair blew over, but raised further questions about Joan's willingness to do any and all work just for the money. In the case of regional theater, one of her concerns must have been the company she'd be keeping: this was the kind of thing that matrons like Lana Turner and June Havoc did. If *that* image were to take hold in Hollywood, she'd really be sunk. Much better to be photographed doing something young, like discoing.

Months before, on May 23, 1976, the following appeared in *Parade* magazine, obviously written by someone who had managed to miss her on *Police Woman* or one of her other small-time TV appearances:

Q: What has happened to that lovely actress Joan Collins?
A: Still as hauntingly beautiful as she was twenty years ago, Joan, like most actresses, finds good roles are few and far between. Her latest plan is to star in *The Stud*, a movie based on one of the series of highly spiced novels written by her sister Jackie, who is emerging as a kind of British Jacqueline Susann.

* * *

While Joan was busy floundering in Britain and then in Hollywood, Jackie had been putting her years of observing the entertainment scene to good use. As a wife and mother, she started writing in her spare time. The hallmark of her books was not just the rich and powerful, but how the young and/or ambitious interact with the czars in their field. "I write books that I would like to pick up myself at the airport and read," she has stated. "Fast reads that are fun."

Jackie wrote *The Stud* in 1969, one of the tawdriest and least literate novels to come along in many a day—right down to incomplete sentences like, "That bloody bitch Fontaine was a real balls breaker, and her skinny friend—Miss No Tits society bag," and "Wispy hair, boobies flopping in a chiffon dress." No matter. It sold well, and Joan felt it would make a successful movie with her in the lead. Putting up a determined front, she said, "I've realized that for an actress to sit and wait for the phone to ring so that your producer friend can say, 'Joan—Anne Bancroft, Jane Fonda, Shirley MacLaine, and Faye Dunaway have turned this movie down so we now want you' is unrealistic. So I want to get myself into a position to be able to create property ideas for myself which will fulfill me creatively."

For all her high-minded rhetoric, Joan knew that creative fulfillment was not something that a film version of *The Stud* would give her. Jackie's story tells of the conjugal adventures of Tony Blake, who runs a disco called Hobo for the wealthy Khaleds, Benjamin and his thirty-five-year-old wife, ex-model Fontaine. Fontaine has a ravenous sexual appetite, which Blake is able to sate; so thrilled is she with him, in fact, that she insists on sharing him with others. Eventually, Benjamin finds out about them and divorces Fontaine, whose saga continued in another of Jackie's thin sexual romps.

The Stud was not the stuff of art. Joan tried to put a good face on it, saying that *The Stud* was really "a modern love story, and in love stories today the boy and girl don't go out holding hands into the sunset." However, her defense rang hollow, as even she had to admit. "I knew what I was doing when I got into *The Stud*," she confessed to columnist James Cameron-Wilson. "I knew I was going to have to exploit myself and commercialize myself, take off my clothes and do all the things that I have studiously avoided in films for years." Joan knew that if she and Kass were going to be able to raise money to make the picture, sex and nudity were a necessary selling point.

Jackie wrote a script—"Joan's career was in a slump," she says, "[so] I did it for nothing"—and, between acting assignments, Joan took the project to every studio and independent producer who would see her. Jackie kept Joan's resolve up by reminding her, "You're only good when you play bitches." At one point toward the end of 1976 it actually looked as though the picture was going to get off the ground, with singer Tom Jones as the stud. But that fell through, and proved to be as close as she would get in Hollywood. For while few producers were averse to making trash, they tended to draw the line at soft-core pornography.

Eventually, *The Stud* would be made. All it took was perseverence and, ironically, *Empire of the Ants*.

Chapter Twenty-one

◆◆◆

*I*n January, after making *Empire of the Ants*, and shortly before beginning a classy remake of *The Big Sleep*, Joan took a vacation in Acapulco—no doubt a gallant effort to collect her strength for the play date in Chicago. (Though she often cried poverty, Joan always found money to pamper herself when it came to clothes and travel, which she admitted were her two vices. She justified these extravagances by stating that they gave her "all the more impetus for making more money.")

The trip to Acapulco was not extraordinary except that, while she was there, Joan began jotting down notes about the highs and lows of her life. Her primary motivation, she says, was "sheer boredom, for a start." She thought that writing an autobiography would help her to feel less "like a book on a library shelf, waiting to be borrowed" between films. Apart from that, she wanted to set a record straight on two counts. First, she happened to go through a lot of press clippings that had piled up and says, "When I reread them I *blanched*. I absolutely *blanched*. I came across as a total ding-a-ling." Second, and more important, because of her husbands and many boyfriends, "Everybody used to think I was the Playgirl of the Western World. I wanted to prove that there is more to me than that."

Joan worked on the material over the next few months, expanding its scope and adding pithy comments. When she had about 60,000 words, she decided to see if they were worth publishing. The manuscript was turned over to legendary agent Irving "Swifty" Lazar, who sent it to W. H. Allen, English publishers. Although *The Stud* had yet to be released, they saw the commercial potential in Joan's candid (read: hot) confessional about her lovers, her films, and her life, and decided they would publish *Past Imperfect* in 1978.

Upon hearing the news, one British newspaper warned, "Men, stand by your lawyers. Keep your wife away from the bookstore. Miss Collins has just sold her life story." Of course, Joan didn't see it that way, and seemed annoyed that so many journalists were harping on the playgirl image that she was trying to dispel. But she would endure it for now, hoping that the book itself would dispel her lingering tart image—never imagining that even hotter press lay ahead.

Joan made three films in 1977. The least significant of these was the Italian *Poliziotto Senza Paura* (*Policeman Without Fear*), and the most successful was *The Stud*. However, the best of them was *The Big Sleep*, a remake of the Raymond Chandler mystery which originally starred Humphrey Bogart as Philip Marlowe.

Directed by Michael Winner (*Death Wish*), this version of *The Big Sleep* was shot in England and has Marlowe (Robert Mitchum) searching for a missing man and becoming embroiled with a pornographer (Edward Fox) and his promiscuous killer/model (Candy Clark). Also featured in the film are James Stewart, Oliver Reed, John Mills, and Sarah Miles.

Joan co-stars as the quiet but grasping Agnes Lozelle, the receptionist at an upscale bookshop which fronts for the dirty book trade. She is snide but poised and has, as Marlowe puts it, "Enough sex appeal to stampede a businessman's lunch." Agnes is not, however, at all licentious; the only relationship she has with Marlowe is trading' information for money. Joan conveys her sex appeal by what obviously lurks below the surface; the only time she lets on that there's an itchy, impatient woman beneath her conservative wardrobe is when she loses just a *little* control, drumming her silver fingernails on a desktop—slowly, rhythmically, sensuously. It's a marvelously restrained performance, arguably the best of Joan's career.

"Joan is a good actress, an underrated actress," says Winner. "And I think she realized that playing a calculating, low-keyed villainess, she didn't have to go at full blast. She could, for once, play it understated."

The Big Sleep is a taut, well-made film, though it was generally panned and not widely seen upon its release. Unfortunately, it was critized less for its own few failings than for the fact that it dared to be a remake of a classic. (Says Winner: "I took the view that *Hamlet*'s been done more than once, so what the hell?") But Joan received good reviews, and it's interesting to speculate on whether or not she could have enjoyed a creative renaissance if she hadn't perpetuated the sexpot image by making *The Stud*.

Winner believes it would have been possible. "She has said that that was a kind of rebirth of her career, that she'd been doing rather grubby 'B' pictures, and this was more elegant employment among very important artists." He says that to have gone from *The Big Sleep* to a picture where she was "swinging on a swing with her tits out" may have made commercial sense but, ultimately, hampered her development as an artist.

Still, he says that during the making of *The Big Sleep* she was the epitome of cooperation and diligence. "She was a great professional, no trouble at all. The only problem I had was that she often wears a wig, and I said, 'No, you mustn't wear a wig. I *hate* wigs.'" She agreed not to wear it, says Winner, and when her last scene was shot, she "showed him" by "pulling at her hair, and off came the wig. She'd been wearing it the whole time." While Winner says it didn't affect the picture adversely, it *is* an example of the lazy Joan—the woman who likes to be able to leave her hair at the studio; have it set, then simply slip into it the next morning without sitting for hours in the hairdresser's chair.

In May 1977, at the behest of American International, Joan went to the Cannes Film Festival to promote *Empire of the Ants*. She didn't want to do it, but also didn't want to offend Samuel Arkoff, the head of AIP, lest the company not give her any more work.

While she was with Arkoff at one of the affairs, Joan was introduced to George Walker, a film distributor who was interested in getting into production. Joan didn't need an engraved invitation. Taking Walker aside, she pitched *The Stud*, and within a matter of days had a deal. Shooting would commence later in the summer, with Walker's company Brent-Walker putting up the money, and Kass serving as one of the producers.

At once, a multinational talent hunt was launched to find the Stud. Given legitimate casting searches for characters as extraordinary as Scarlett O'Hara and Annie, the quest for the Stud was unintentionally comical. Just how good an actress Joan is becomes clear by the way she was able to talk straight-faced to the press about how they looked long and hard for a man who not only could act but was so dynamic that he had the ladies "falling at his feet and at his fly." In the end, after discarding stunning Italian actors whose accent was too thick, and "guys who had more sex appeal but . . . didn't have the experience," they settled on Oliver Tobias. No doubt the real consideration was that he came relatively cheap, since when Tobias wasn't taking Joan in the elevator, in bed, or on the aforementioned swing, he brought little talent and surprisingly less charisma to the part.

Not that Joan was much better. Lines like "All of Tony's zones are errogenous" and "Ben gets his cock sucked once a month, always in the dark, and never in the lift," hardly leave room for nuance. In any case, Joan's explicit sex scenes and nudity—full frontal and otherwise—were what brought people into the theaters, not characterization. And bring in the customers it did. When *The Stud* opened in England in the spring, it fast became one of the biggest hits in recent British film history. "And suddenly," says Joan triumphantly, "I was a big star in England again."

Joan took a great deal of critical heat for having made such a lurid picture, especially for the orgy scene in which she hopped on the swing and went sailing over a pool full of writhing bodies. That is the only scene she refuses to defend. She felt uncomfortable with it from the start, and wanted to wear a towel, but Kass said "it was a copout. He tells me I have a great body, so what the hell?" But it got worse once they started shooting. Says Joan, "Usually when you do a nude scene, it's just you and another actor on a closed set, with a few crew people and a screen around the camera. But the orgy was shot at a completely open pool, so there was no way to block the technicians." In order to do the scene, Joan says she got drunk—which only made things worse, since she "did things I normally wouldn't do."

However, she refused to apologize for anything else that was in the film. Sometimes she was defensive, remarking, "I don't think I lowered my standards doing the picture because I don't have the same hangups about nudity and sex that a lot of people do." She would later opine that "getting stabbed like Angie Dickenson did in *Dressed to Kill* is *much* more demeaning that being naked in a movie. I don't think it's wrong to show the body." Sometimes she got indignant, saying, "I can't understand why people pan me for nudity when Glenda Jackson and Jane

Fonda have done the same thing in their pictures"—
Joan showing remarkable brass, if little insight, by
putting *The Stud* in the same class as *Women in Love*
and *Coming Home*.

Yet years later, when the need for money was no
longer urgent, and her fame was secure, she said
more objectively, "*The Stud* relaunched my career, I'd
be a fool to regret that. [But] exploiting myself was a
mistake." She admitted that undraping her forty-five-
year-old body and parading it around may have done
some good "for my own self-esteem," but, as Winner
said, it set her thespian aspirations back to square
one.

Also, while it made Joan a big star, *The Stud* did not
make her a wealthy star. She had gotten £25,000 to
make the picture, and Kass had gotten a matching
sum to produce it. Says Kass, "Joan also did all she
could to promote it, making personal appearances,
appearing on chat shows, and giving endless interviews." But while he says that the movie's dis-
tributors "boasted that *The Stud* had made millions"—the $600,000 picture took in over $20 million
even *before* it came to the U.S.—he and Joan got only
"a tiny percentage of the film's gigantic profits."
Eventually, Joan and her husband went to court to try
to get what they felt was their fair share not only of
the theatrical revenues in England and the U.S.
(where it opened in September 1979, after being
judiciously edited to avert an "X" rating) but of the
monumental sales and rentals of the videocassette in
both countries. It was, however, an exercise in
futility. To make matters worse, virtually every penny
they had been given up-front on the film went into
legal fees and airfare between the U.S. and England
to fight the case. Thus, lamented Kass, while "it
could have been the big one—so much so that neither
of us would have to worry about money again—
instead it became a millstone round our necks."

Chapter Twenty-two

❖❖❖❖❖❖❖❖❖❖❖❖❖❖❖❖❖❖❖❖❖❖❖❖❖❖❖❖❖❖❖❖❖❖❖❖

While awaiting the re-
lease of *The Stud*, Joan knocked out a pair of abysmal
quickies: *Zero to 60* and *Game for Vultures*, filmed in
Los Angeles and South Africa, respectively. The
latter, co-starring Richard Harris and Ray Milland, is
a convoluted but respectable action film, but *Zero to
60*, starring Darren McGavin, is one of the most
moronic movies ever made, featuring a plot about a
ring of car thieves. Joan's role makes no sense
whatsoever. She is the owner of a silver Trans-Am
and spends the entire movie running from one of the
thieves (a teenage girl) who wants her car—popping
in and out of the film with no character development
at all, and having an affair with McGavin for no
apparent reason. Even the car chases are pedestrian.

Joan also made a picture called *Homework*, which
didn't open until August 1982, at which time controversy would surround the film. *Homework* is a
surprisingly witty soft-core porn movie about a teenager named Tommy (Michael Morgan) who is desperately trying to lose his virginity. Joan, who worked
only three days on the film, is briefly seen as Diane,
the mother of Tommy's inattentive girlfriend. Diane,
who is herself sexually frustrated, finally seduces the
youth while he's standing on a ladder hanging a
painting for her. The sequence may not be art, but
Joan makes it a masterpiece of desire as she starts and
stops and finally decides to run her hands along his

legs. A stand-in was used for shots of Diane and Tommy naked in bed.

The controversy arose when Joan became a household name due to *Dynasty* and Jensen Farley Pictures released *Homework* with ads which not only put Joan's name above the title but showed her barely clad. Since she was in the film for about ten minutes, she resented the way her name was being exploited; worse, the nude shot was misleading since she hadn't done any nude scenes in the film. The ad was created by putting her face atop another woman's body. Joan went to court to have the advertising changed, and won. She was joined in her complaint by actress Carrie Snodgrass, who played a psychologist in the film; Betty Thomas (of *Hill Street Blues*) also wanted her name taken off the film. Both claimed to have had no idea they were making a movie of such a sensational nature.

Hollywood may have been where most of the work was, but both *The Stud*, her most successful picture, and *The Big Sleep*, her most artistic, had been made in England; clearly, London was the place to be. On top of that, *Past Imperfect* would be edited and published in England. Since Kass no longer had to be in Los Angeles—and was, in fact, doing better in England— they decided to move back.

Much to Joan's unspeakable disappointment, when she and Kass elected to resettle in England, only Katy went with them. Tara and Sacha elected not to go, moving in with father Newley.

"Apparently," Joan said bitterly, "I wasn't a fit mother, leading a flighty actress life. This person who takes her clothes off on film." Though Joan has never said anything more about it, this move was apparently caused by embarrassment with *The Stud*, since the publication of *Past Imperfect*—which could not have helped the situation—was still several months in the future. In any event, their decision was devastating to her. "I didn't crack up," Joan says, "or have a nervous breakdown or anything. I carried on more or less normally. But the strain came out in my skin. I got spots. Dozens and dozens of them. There was nothing I could do that would make them go away. Doctors said that only when my problems cleared up would the spots go."

Her problems didn't clear up for nearly a year, the children coming back in July 1979. Yet their absence wasn't the only emotional drain on Joan during that period. Though she reveled in the success of *The Stud* and managed to weather the criticism, the subsequent publication of *Past Imperfect* made *that* storm seem like a drizzle.

As soon as the book was published, Joan found herself using the same kind of defensive tactics she'd been forced to employ on *The Stud*. She tried to show that her book was not the nonfiction counterpart of the trash her sister writes. "It was more a catharsis project for me. I'd always been somewhat juvenile in my attitude to life, letting myself be carried on by advice from others. My aim was to get to know myself." Sometimes she'd try to put it forth as a "personal best" kind of effort. "I'm really proud that I wrote the book, because . . . I did it without a ghostwriter." And, she would insist, it was *more* than a book about bed-hopping. "I personally think it's awful for anyone to write a kiss-and-tell book if that's the only reason for writing one." But if reporters didn't buy any of that, she'd bristle right back, exclaiming, "You just can't stand by and let the world kick you in the teeth. I will *not* let myself be maligned or victimized." She said that the book was as candid as it was because "I couldn't write a story about my life without mentioning that I had relationships with men who were instrumental in influencing my life and career. It would have been a total copout if I left out the names." Of course she did leave out the names of Harry Belafonte and George Englund in the book's British publication, making for only a partial copout.

For all the critical lambasting she took for her candor in recounting her affairs and some of her darker emotions, the book is extremely entertaining, written in sharp, lively language that is pure Joan Collins. As an author, she is both vivid and amusing. However, as a *nonfiction* author, Joan leaves a lot to be desired. She has confessed, elsewhere, that she has "terrible, diabolical memory [for] things in the past," and it shows.

While many of the errors (factual and chronological) should have been caught in the editing process, the mistakes do not speak well for Joan's interest in accuracy. Then, too, she is understandably selective when discussing her own failings. Typical is the way she blames the fact that her children moved in with Newley solely on her constantly having to work and being away, never once even alluding to any possible negative reaction to the public spectacle she had managed to make of herself. And while she mentions most of her films, *The Executioner* is conspicuous by its absence. As Joan told Johnny Carson one night, the book is "about the good and bad things I did; mostly good." Certainly *she* regarded herself as good. But inaccuracies aside, her views are annoyingly selective and incomplete—most notably about Maxwell Reed, Anthony Newley, and Bert I. Gordon. Whatever Joan learned about herself by writing the book, she did not always share it with her readers.

The book was a best seller in England, and Joan was delighted that of all the people she discussed in often intimate detail, "the only man I know who has been upset by it was Newley." However, she added, "Since we weren't talking before it came out, there was no reason that we'd be talking afterward." He later said more pointedly, "We haven't been [on speaking terms] for over a decade. We do not like each other at all." Warner Books was impressed enough with the revelations in the autobiography to feel that *Past Imperfect* would be a success in the U.S.

as well and they advanced her $100,000 to publish the memoirs in 1979. However, as the months passed and Joan was able to assimilate the reaction, she began to have second thoughts. "I wrote the book to set the record straight," she sighed, "but it's rather backfired in that all it's really done is drag everything up again. When it was published in England I went through misery, sneers, and jests," she says, and worried, "If this is how my own countrymen reacted, how would Americans react? I couldn't face it and turned back the advance."

Until she had a change of heart and an edited and embellished edition was published by Simon & Schuster, not by Warner, to great success in 1984—immediately soaring to the top of U.S. best-seller lists—copies of *Past Imperfect* were, according to the *Daily News*, "a choice black market item."

The horror industry had shifted from England to Hollywood when *The Exorcist* opened in 1973, and the U.S. continued to dominate the field with the more explicit "splatter" films. The genre where Joan had so often found gainful employment was no more, and it was once again catch-as-catch-can. Unfortunately, Britain was in a worse slump than ever: most of the films being made there were U.S. productions such as *Superman, Alien*, and *The Empire Strikes Back*. Though the crews were largely British, the leading actors were American.

Except for television, which she did on occasion, and a supporting part in Farrah Fawcett's theatrical flop, *Sunburn*, there wasn't much for Joan to do. Thus, Jackie served up a sequel to *The Stud*. Entitled *The Bitch*, this one continued the adventures of Fontaine Khaled. She's still, in Joan's words, "a power-hungry nymphomaniac," this time trying to revitalize the failing Hobo disco, which she'd gotten from her ex-husband. Concurrently, she becomes involved with the mob when, unknown to Fontaine, a hustler named Nico Costofora slips a hot gem into her white fox cape. Though Joan wasn't fond of the Brent-Walker team because of the ongoing financial row, *The Bitch* rolled late in 1979.

While Joan had managed to find brave things to say about *The Stud*, she found it impossible to praise *The Bitch*. "I *hate* it," she says forthrightly, "it was a bad movie." And it was a bad movie, just like *The Stud*. The dialogue remained as idiotically licentious and awkward as before ("What would you imagine me in the sack," Fontaine asks her chauffeur, "fucking like rattlesnakes?"), there was another pool orgy— though without the swing and, hence, its cinemato- graphic possibilities—and breasts were bared at every opportunity, Joan's among countless others.

When the picture was released at year's end, the public ate it up while Joan talked it down. "I should have refused to do it," she sniffed. "It wasn't ready to shoot. They didn't have a proper script, a decent director, or a leading man. I should have put my foot down." Demonstrating the syndrome described by Bert Gordon, she painted a public portrait of herself as a well-meaning actress who had been abused by money-hungry producers. Brimming with righteous indignation, she said she made *The Bitch* only because she was contractually obligated—even though it was a matter of record that she'd refused countless films at Fox when she was "contractually obligated" there. Actually Joan knew *exactly* what kind of a picture it was and, for their part, the producers rightly felt that esthetics didn't matter: they had just the script and all the bodies they wanted. More than likely, it wasn't the contract that prompted Joan to make the film, but the money she got for starring and Kass for co- producing. For though she tried to put herself on the high road by declaring "I think people are bored with sex films and all that huffing and puffing onscreen," she wasn't quite as indignant as her negativism suggests—a theory supported by the fact that *The*

Bitch was not the last piece of exploitation she'd end up doing.

For what it was worth, *The Bitch* did manage to give Joan a first. A photo of her dressed in a corset and garter belt, mink draped around her shoulders, chauffeur's cap on her hair, head cocked seductively to one side, became one of the most enduring icons of the late seventies. At forty-six, Joan had managed to equal a feat which previously had been the dominion of youngsters like Farrah Fawcett and the Dallas Cowboy Cheerleaders. Secretly, she could not have helped but be satisfied by that.

Unlike America, Britain gave Joan some quality work to do on TV during this period, most notably in a trio of episodes on the British-made anthology series *Tales of the Unexpected*. However, because of her newfound notoriety, even a simple TV show in which Joan was appearing found a way to make news. In one such episode Joan played a grim but interesting villainess: a mother who falls under the influence of a mad clergyman and is compelled to eat her children. There was a scene in which her character and other women in the cast were to appear nude from the waist up. To make matters worse, the scene was to be shot in a church in Norfolk. Though a double was to be used for Joan, and the actresses would be shot only from behind, when the Bishop of Norwich learned what was going on he squelched the shoot. It was done, instead, in an old crypt, but not before making headlines like "JOAN DRIVES THE VICAR CRAZY."

Joan also kept busy during 1979 writing a book of grooming and fitness tips for working women. "People kept asking me: 'How do you manage to go on looking like that at your age?' So I said to my agent that maybe I should write a book about it. A week later I'd signed the contract." She said she had a great deal of sympathy for the plight of the today's woman since, when she had a late call or wasn't shooting,

Joan took the children to school each morning. "Men only have to worry about work," she said, "[while] women have to work and do the homekeeping at the same time. I've managed to do it [with the help of nannies, it should be pointed out] and keep myself in trim. I've picked up a lot of tips which might help working women to look good for themselves and not necessarily for men."

However, her book was not like the others that were just beginning to flood the market. "Most beauty books are written like lacrosse manuals," she said. "They're very complicated, such as making something as ordinary as a beauty mask. 'Take three carnations and put them in a blender with the juice of four cucumbers and a bit of yogurt,'" she mimicked, in the style of these books. "'Put it in the refrigerator for three days and strain it through a cheesecloth before putting it on your face. Now that kind of thing is ridiculous. My book is done in a straightforward way."

Well, *almost* straightforward. She still managed to set herself apart from the average lady, and reinforce her image as a dazzling bastion of youth and vitality, by dedicating the book to what London's *Sunday Telegraph* magazine described as "the guest list for a jet-set children's tea party," with nods to the daughters of friend Roger Moore, Juliet Mills, the Bricusses, and others.

The Joan Collins Beauty Book was published at the year's end in England, accompanied by the arranging of Joan Collins manikins in store windows and, like her previous book, became a best seller, albeit not for the same reasons. The irony of her success as an author cannot have escaped Joan. While she was able to succeed with a pair of totally different books, the only time her film career ever really took off in a quarter-century was when she played some kind of tramp. Kass had been close to putting together a deal for *The Lady and the Champ*, in which she would have played the classy wife of a government official, but that fell through, "helped" by a flood of press in England which made the words "Joan Collins" and "Bitch" synonymous, and she was more strongly typecast now than she'd been in her Rank days.

As the year drew to a close, Joan resolved to try to change her image by eating crow and taking some old RADA advice—by boldly going onto the London stage.

Chapter Twenty-three

Joan was able to go back on the stage for barely a living wage because she had managed to build herself a good monetary base. While she had not received as much as she felt she deserved from *The Stud* and *The Bitch*, Joan was receiving some £20,000 a year from a series of now-legendary TV comercials for Cinzano.

She was in California the year before when the Collett, Dickinson, Pearce agency contacted her about doing comercials for the vermouth. Joan was reluctant at first. She was just in from London for a visit and not anxious to turn right around; moreover, she had not heard of Leonard Rossiter, the actor with whom she would be co-starring. Finally, after *The Stud*, TV commercials might well destroy what was left of her credibility as an actress. "Then," she says, "they sent me some scripts. I read them, found them hilarious, and decided to give it a whirl."

It was, as it turned out, one of the wisest moves she ever made. The essence of the campaign was to poke fun at the rich snob crowd in which Fontaine Khaled moved. At the end of the spots, the ritzy Joan would end up having a glass of Cinzano spilled down her front. Fontaine Khaled had been played with such leering sobriety that the commercials would prove Joan capable of much more. "I learnt to send myself up," she said of the advertisements. And when she flew back to make the first of them, she was delighted to discover "some kind of chemistry working between Leonard and myself." She was also pleased to find that in advertising, it was necessary to use the product, not a substitute, when filming. "There's an official present to make sure we drink the real stuff," she said, "so by eleven o'clock in the morning we can be quite squiffed. We drink an awful lot of black coffee too."

The first spot was a hit, additional ones were made, and Joan was signed for even more. In fact, so well received was the Collins-Rossiter team that screenwriters Ian le Frenais and Dick Clements were hired to develop the theme into a feature-length theatrical film.

(Alas, the spots were killed by Cinzano after three years. While the public loved them, Cinzano executives finally concluded that it wasn't a good idea to make fun of their product. Although Joan, finally having been able to do the kind of comedy she relished, was "shattered," by that time she had a more lucrative project in which to lose herself—*Dynasty*. For now, however, she had a financial cushion and was able to devote herself to the theater.)

At first, she had planned to make her debut in January 1980 in Noel Coward's *Design for Living*. But that project fell through and Joan rescheduled her return to the stage as part of the summer slate at the Chichester Festival Arts Theater. This time the vehicle was the 1925 Frederick Lonsdale comedy, *The Last of Mrs. Cheyney*.

When the play opened, it received scathing reviews. Joan was upset and certainly more than a little shaken to be slammed on her return. However, the box office was excellent through the July and August run, and Joan said gallantly, "The show put bums on seats, which is what matters. Besides, I've always been critic fodder. They don't like me."

Although there were better stage actresses than Joan, there was some truth in what she said. Michael Winner, a longtime Joan Collins booster, explains the problem with the press is that "a prophet is never a prophet in his or her own land. I think the press thought Joan was a little gaudy and spangly. Well, the British like their licentious free spirits to be foreign. It's all right if they're French or Italian or American, but if they're English it's rather like they're letting the side down."

Joan toughed it out and, much to her satisfaction, the show proved so profitable that while it was still running she and Kass were approached by Triumph Productions to bring the play to the West End in October. The prospect of playing in the heart of London caused Joan both pleasure and trepidation. There were few mountains higher than that for an actor to climb, and she was game. But Joan also knew she would probably be destroyed all over again by the press, more harshly, if possible, because she was aspiring to the big time. That was a very unpleasant prospect, but Kass helped her to look beyond opening night. He felt that there was a fortune to be made in a successful run, and she anxiously accepted, the couple even putting a chunk of their own money into the show.

To ensure the play's financial well-being, Kass and Triumph's Duncan Weldon planned a complex and resourceful multimedia promotional blitz. Said an excited Kass, "If anything, Joan's visibility will be stronger than for *The Stud*, when we felt we were lucky with a book tie-in [*Past Imperfect*]. For this play we are into bookstores, record stores, print, radio, films, and in several forms of TV promotion."

The linchpin of their efforts was the beauty book, and Joan would indeed be everywhere: pushing the book when it was published in October and serialized in the *Daily Mail*. It was heard in homes on a spoken word version from Warwick Records and seen on Yellowbill Productions' video version, which would be aired as a special and released as a tape. Meanwhile, Brent-Walker would be reissuing *The Bitch* theatrically on a double bill with, appropriately enough, Warren Beatty's *Shampoo*. Cinzano, which had not yet given up on her ads, agreed to increase the frequency of their airing. There would be a new push for the videocassette versions of both *The Stud* and, when its theatrical reissue was completed, *The Bitch*. "This is not just exploitation," Kass pointed out, "it's good promotion."

Then, as it always seemed to do when Joan was getting on a roll, the bandwagon came to a cataclysmic halt.

On August 1, 1980, Joan and Ron went to Paris to confer with a costume designer about the more elaborate wardrobe their West End production would require. Tara, never having seen Paris, went with them; eight-year-old Katy was left at their Mayfair home with nanny Fiona Aitken.

While Katy was visiting with a girlfriend in rustic Berkshire, she, her friend Georgina, and Georgina's eleven-year-old cousin were playing tag. But the boy got tired of the game and left; the two girls chased after him, following him through the garden and onto an unpaved street. Their hands were locked, and neither saw the oncoming car. The driver, eighteen years old, was driving twenty-seven miles an hour in the thirty-mile-an-hour zone, and though he braked and tried not to hit them, it wasn't possible. Georgina's leg was broken in three places but Katy got the worst of it, being hit by the bumper and thrown back, striking her head against the curb.

Fortunately, the young driver was a nurse. Additional help was summoned but, because Katy had obviously suffered brain injury, the decision was made not to place her in a local hospital but to risk transporting her by ambulance to the better-equipped Central Middlesex Hospital just west of London.

Meanwhile, Joan was contacted in Paris. It was 2:00 A.M. and when the call came Joan was like a lunatic, wailing hysterically—not only was her baby hurt but she, unable to get a commercial flight, was helplessly stranded hundreds of miles away. Later, commenting on the night, Joan quietly stated that she was "the most upset I've ever been."

Fortunately, a friend with a plane volunteered to fly Joan, Ron, and Tara to London. Upon arriving at the hospital's intensive care unit, the Kasses were met by a chilling sight: Katy was hooked to a life-support system, tubes in her nose, wrists, and throat. Her hair had been cut off entirely, and her skin was a pasty color.

Joan walked over and, swallowing tears, bent and clasped Katy's hand in hers. The girl's eyes were closed, but when Joan asked her to squeeze back she did. Though the doctors gave the girl only a 40 percent chance of surviving, Joan knew then that she'd pull through, that something "from the depths of her being" was reaching out, struggling to live. What Joan didn't know was whether or not Katy would be the girl she had always been, or impaired— unable to walk or speak or laugh.

So that they could be around Katy at all times, Joan and Kass moved into a small room in the hospital. During this time, she decided to keep a diary, not with the intention of publishing it but to help her sort out her own thoughts and keep busy during a time of plodding inactivity. When she wasn't writing in it, she spent her time talking to Katy; it didn't matter to

Joan whether or not her daughter could answer. She knew that Katy could *hear* her and Joan wanted to "try to keep active that part of her brain which was still working."

According to Joan's diary, by August 5, the third day of Katy's stay, her doctor saw "a flicker" of improvement, and by the sixth day he took her off the ventilating machine—though there were surgeons on hand to perform an emergency tracheotomy if necessary. It wasn't necessary, and Katy finally breathed on her own. Joan wrote in her diary: "I'm still close to tears all the time. Only when I'm with Katy am I completely in control of myself."

By the end of the first week, the hospital needed the room in which Joan and Kass had been staying, so they borrowed a mobile home and moved in next to the building. Throughout, Joan paid absolutely no attention to her appearance. She smoked and drank to give her strength and to keep calm, and noted in her diary, "I don't give a damn who sees me. I only care about pouring all my energy and strength into Katy."

Finally, on the eighth day, Katy opened her eyes. There was, as yet, no expression in them, but it was a quantum leap from where she'd been. Both her parents and the doctor were elated. On that same day, however, Katy stopped breathing due to a muscular spasm and had to be resuscitated. The life-support system to which she was still hooked had, fortunately, sounded the alarm, but thereafter Joan decided that she would stay with Katy all day, and Kass all night.

Joan says of this time, "I am pretty good at coping with life. There have been desperate times before, although nothing quite like this nightmare." One of the worst things about it was the roller-coaster nature of her emotions. She was governed by extremes, clutching like a drowning woman at every sign of improvement, becoming understandably devastated by every discouraging word. Typical was a conversation she had on the tenth day of Katy's hospitalization. A doctor came around and, after listening to Joan burble on about how thrilled she was with Katy's progress, casually informed her that she "mustn't get *too* optimistic, as the chances are strong that she will have some disability." Hearing this, Joan notes in her diary that she struggled to keep from crying as she made her way to the trailer, where she "beat the hell out of it. I hit and punched the walls and the pillows and the bed until my knuckles bled, and screamed my head off with the anger and pent-up frustration of it all."

Meanwhile, mail from sympathetic fans and supportive parents helped keep her sane. "I have had so many letters from mothers who have been through this thing," she said during Katy's stay, "telling me what to expect and how to cope. I have contacted three of the mothers and talked things over with them. 'Don't expect her eyes to be dancing with light and vitality,' they told me." But they reinforced her conviction that she must stay with Katy whenever possible. "Everyone who has experienced this says the same thing. You must keep giving some kind of stimulus, even if she isn't responding."

Joan says that in addition to drawing on the experiences of others, two more factors helped her "face up to the long process of bringing Katy back." One was her Actualization training, which allowed Joan to focus her energies; another was a psychic dug up by Rod Stewart's wife. Joan said solemnly, "Alana rang me from California to tell me that she had talked to a psychic about Katy. Later I talked to the psychic myself. She told me Katy would get better, but would need a lot of help and rehabilitation." It was nothing Joan didn't know, but it was nice to hear it from one who was allegedly in touch with the future.

During her second week in the hospital, Katy was moved to the children's ward, where the environment was far less oppressive for Joan and Ron. Within days, Katy had moved her right leg—involuntarily at first, then "on command." Joan was ecstatic, and worked diligently with Katy until the young girl was able to move her left leg as well. There was also more life in Katy's face, and though she was far from out of the woods, Joan was seeing progress daily and beginning to feel as if a monumental weight were being lifted from her.

As it was now just about six weeks before *The Last of Mrs. Cheyney* was slated to open at the Cambridge Theater, just a few blocks northeast of Leicester Square, a decision had to be made on what to do about the show. Despite having put on weight and letting her appearance go to hell—she had barely bothered to brush her teeth during the past two weeks, let alone her hair—Joan was torn. She wrote in her diary; "As much as I know I *should* work, the thing uppermost in my mind is Katy's welfare and I cannot, and will not, leave her."

After consulting with her agent, she decided to allow the producers to continue with the set-building and costuming, but would wait awhile longer before making a final decision. Only after three weeks, when the still-sluggish Katy was nonetheless able to take solid foods and was finally decatheterized did Joan feel comfortable enough to go ahead with the show.

Against all odds, and faster than even the most optimistic reports had predicted, Katy was on the mend. Though it remained to be seen just how far she would go, signs were good for a near-complete recovery.

All seemed well again, which is when Ron Kass started to show curious signs of decay and Joan's marriage began to unravel.

Chapter Twenty-four

◆◆◆◆◆◆◆◆◆◆◆◆◆◆◆◆◆◆◆◆◆◆◆◆◆◆◆◆◆◆◆◆◆

After six weeks in the hospital, the doctors had done all they could for Katy. Although she was extremely emaciated and still unable to speak, she was moving most of her body and reacting, albeit dully, to sounds, sights, touch, smells, and other stimuli. It was the physiotherapists' turn to work with her, which meant there was no reason for Katy to remain in the hospital. Joan and Ron were allowed to take her home, the doctors feeling that her own bed and familiar surroundings would be the best remedy.

Since it was just three weeks until *The Last of Mrs. Cheyney* opened, Joan had to devote herself almost entirely to the play. That left Kass home-tied, not only during the run of the show but, as it turned out, while Joan went to work on other projects immediately thereafter. Joan said later, "Ron gave up everything. He was involved in various projects, but for a year he spent all day with Katy, helping to nurse her back to health. Because I was working, I was tired, so I was able to sleep. Ron couldn't."

She says, "While all this was going on, he put on about fifteen pounds in weight." Barry Langford, the young man who headed Joan's fan club and served as her part-time secretary, elaborates that before long Kass's favorite meals had become "chocolate bars— which he ate for breakfast, dinner, and tea— interspersed with hamburgers or hot dogs. He and

Joan used to have terrible rows over his eating habits." Had she known what lay ahead, Joan might have been content not to assail his diet.

One of the reasons Joan elected to go ahead with the West End opening was that the special care Katy required ate deeply into her financial cushion. More as an investor than as the star, it was important to her that the show go on and succeed. She got herself into shape, giving up alcohol, losing weight, and working hard with her co-stars to iron out some of the problems critics had found in the first staging. Despite the anguish she still felt inside over Katy, she put on a happy front and did promotions for the show. She'd go on the air or talk to journalists and say breezy things about the play. She'd still have to defend the work she'd done in *The Stud* and *The Bitch*, but she was getting good at it: "By becoming a commercial proposition, I can choose my roles" became something of a standard retort which, due to its simplicity and logic, didn't allow the reporter to lay a glove on her.

In short, Joan did everything she could to ensure the show's success during its scheduled three-month run. But it was not to be. The star presence that had dazzled them in the provinces failed to wow them in the sophisticated city, and *The Last of Mrs. Cheyney* was a bomb.

By January 1981, Joan's finances and personal life had reached another valley. She and Kass had kept their home in Beverly Hills, which Joan flew back to sell to make ends meet. While there, she earned money doing a *Fantasy Island* episode playing, of all things, Cleopatra—but she was terribly anxious about keeping up a work flow. Back in England she did another play that spring, *Murder in Mind*, not for the bare-bones salary but to enhance her reputation as an actress and, she hoped, to stimulate good film roles. Nothing happened. Not even when she shaved

five years off her age. In fact, in June, when Adel
Rootstein U.S.A. created a new line of manikins for
store windows in America, they modeled them after
Joan because, said spokesperson Michael Southgate,
of "her beauty and her age. The woman in her forties
buys a lot of clothes." And while it may have been a
backhanded compliment, Joan willingly posed for
sculptor John Taylor for a relatively small fee. If
nothing else, it put her in the windows of stores like
Saks Fifth Avenue and tempered the unpleasant
exposure she was receiving on videocassettes as
Fontaine.

As ever, in spite of her financial condition, Joan
found money to travel, and in July went with Katy
and Kass on a vacation to Spain. Upon her return she
was committed to tour with *Murder in Mind*, which
promised to be relatively lucrative, since name stars
usually drew very well outside London. After that,
Joan would be taking a second stab at the West End
with a belated staging of Coward's *Design for Living*.

While she was in Spain, Joan got a call from Tom
Korman, her agent in Los Angeles. One of the top TV
producers in Hollywood, Aaron Spelling, had an
ailing series on his hands. The show was called
Dynasty and, launched as a midseason replacement
on ABC, it was a *Dallas*-like series about the rich and
powerful. The hub of the empire-building activity
was Blake Carrington (John Forsythe), a Denver-
based oilman; in his orbit were wife Krystle (Linda
Evans), spoiled daughter Fallon (Pamela Sue Martin),
son Steven (Al Corley), Krystle's ex-lover and Carrington employee Matthew Blaisdel (Bo Hopkins),
Matthew's wife Claudia (Pamela Bellwood), who is in
love with Steven, and Fallon's husband Jeff Colby
(John James), among others.

Despite the romantic and financial intrigue, guer-
rilla attacks on oil rigs in the Middle East, Steven's
spicy adventures in a brothel, and the first-season
closer of Blake going on trial for the murder of his

son's gay lover, not only was *Dynasty* not delivering anything near the kinds of ratings CBS was getting on Fridays with *its* wealth-and-corruption sudser *Dallas*, but *Dynasty* was barely holding its own against the movies on CBS and the aging *Quincy* on NBC.

Spelling was not a man to accept failure. He had produced such hit shows as *Charlie's Angels*, *Fantasy Island*, and *The Love Boat*, and intended to do everything possible to save *Dynasty* from sinking. The way to do that, he felt, was by introducing a new character, someone with the same kind of sugar-coated nastiness as *Dallas*'s J. R. Ewing. Instead of a man, however, he wanted a female, a black widow, someone with more sting than bark. He had the character written into the script as Alexis, Blake Carrington's ex-wife, and she would make her debut as a witness for the prosecution at the millionaire's trial.

At first, Spelling went after Sophen Loren, feeling that a name star of her caliber would attract viewers. But she turned him down, and Raquel Welch was sought. But she was not anxious to do series work and so, with a week left before the second season opener went before the cameras, Spelling went after Joan. Thanks to Fontaine Khaled, she had proved she could play an elegant bitch, and that's just what Spelling wanted.

Joan felt a confusion of emotions as she listened to her agent's long-distance description of the part and the terms. "To be honest," she said, "I had never even heard of *Dynasty* before it was offered to me. My agent said it would be a good part, but he says that a lot."

There were countless reasons for and against Joan accepting the series. In the "pro" column, it was excellent exposure and steady work for at least another half season—which was as long as the network's commitment to the series ran. Then, too, as Katy's doctor pointed out when Joan quickly consulted him, the sunny, warm climate of California would be much better for the girl than "the bleak London weather." Though Katy had made excellent progress in the year since her accident, being able to write and get about, she had lingering problems with balance, coordination, memory, and certain fine motor skills. Being able to swim every day and go out during the winter would help her recovery.

On the "con" side, Joan was afraid of viewer backlash. "I don't take parts to win popularity contests," she said, "but I didn't think American audiences would accept a *naughty* lady coming into their homes every week." Offending the public could obviously hurt her career; or, conversely, if they embraced her, Alexis might only serve to reinforce the Fontaine image she'd been trying to shed for years. She'd be typecast for life. Joan was reluctant, too, because she *did* have the play to do, and did not especially want to go back to Los Angeles.

In the end, however, there really wasn't much choice. Encouraged by Kass, who, as it turned out, had his own selfish reasons for wanting her to take *Dynasty*, Joan realized she'd be a fool to turn down the show. Even it it wasn't art, no one was offering her great roles on the screen. And, at worst, she would have an audience each week in the tens of millions—more than she'd *ever* had. She would stop being "Joan who?" in Hollywood, and doors might open for her. Her self-respect was more important than the danger of being typecast.

Within twenty-six hours of receiving Korman's call, Joan was back in Hollywood—though not quite free and clear to do *Dynasty*. Triumph was not at all pleased to be losing Joan for the *Murder in Mind* tour, which would be precluded by her involvement in the TV series. There were some very heated discussions about Joan's breaching her contract, though the lawsuits threatened by both sides never materialized. Joan was replaced by actress Nyree Dawn Porter in *Murder*, thus leaving her free to tackle *Dynasty*.

* * *

After watching tapes of first-season *Dynasty* shows, Joan was convinced that it was going to go to a quick death. Hollywood, however, was of a different mind. The producers and cast alike were looking to her as the savior. She had known that she was supposed to help the show, but *save* it—that was a responsibility on which she hadn't counted. Worse, the first episode featured one of the most difficult kinds of scenes for an actor: a trial. By nature, trials are melodramatic, yet the actor must be careful not to overact; the scenes are usually emotional, so the performer must dip into memories both pleasant and unpleasant to get in the proper frame of mind. Topping it off, the star is being watched by dozens of fellow performers. When those performers are counting on someone to save their jobs by boosting the ratings, the pressure can be awesome.

Joan felt it. The London critics probably wouldn't have appreciated it, but Joan was more anxious performing for Middle America than she had been stepping onstage in the illustrious West End. It was a different kind of anxiety. On the stage, she was reaching for the brass ring of acting and acting alone. Here, everything would be under scrutiny—acting, beauty, poise—and not from afar but in unsympathetic closeups.

And then there was the hype. ABC would be airing promotional spots and taking out print ads emphasizing *her* ("When this women lifts her veil tonight, will Blake Carrington be condemned for murder?").

If ever the heat was on, it was on the morning Joan left her trailer at, of all places, the Fox Studios.

She was wearing a hat with a wide brim—a look overpowering for most women, but not for Alexis. A thin veil hung from the brim, behind which she wore large, round sunglasses. The hat was white with a black band; her white blazer had jet black lapels and buttons. She moved with the self-assurance of a tigress, and while dear Claudia may have been recovering from a near-fatal automobile accident, and Krystle may have been having frightening dizzy spells, when Alexis Carrington took the stand, she was unarguably the star and focus of *Dynasty*.

Alexis was grilled. She talked about how she and Blake had a good marriage, at first. Two beautiful children. Then it spoiled. Blake became preoccupied with business, with building his dynasty. She strayed, found another man. Blake screamed oaths at her. He divorced Alexis and threatened her with disfigurement if she ever came back. She recalled for the court the horror of the encounter.

Joan was rolling: it was a character she understood. She was cool as she discussed her first marriage. Bittersweet as she recounted the good years. Embarrassed and hesitant as she confessed the affair. Sweetly vindictive as she talked about Blake's threats. And positively carnivorous as she engaged her livid ex-husband in chitchat after her testimony, her blood-red lips bent in a cruel, triumphant smile. As the episode ended just before the announcing of the verdict, it was clear to Hollywood and to televiewers across the country that this English has-been had risen to the challenge, coming from the bench and saving the day for *Dynasty*.

Blake Carrington was convicted of involuntary manslaughter and given a two years suspended sentence. But after her dirty deed was done, Alexis decided to stay in Denver rather than return to Acapulco: the better to meddle in Carrington family matters. To the delight of an ever-increasing audience, in the weeks that followed Alexis and the other Carringtons wrestled with the question of whether Blake was *really* Fallon's father, the nature of Steven's accident in the pool, Blake's ill-advised dealings with a Las Vegas gangster, Krystle's pregnancy, Alexis's freeing of Blake's embargoed oil and their cozy tête-à-tête in Rome, trouble with the gangsters and their attempt on Blake's life, a spectacular crime commission hearing, Blake's blindness, Fallon's pregnancy, Alexis's alleged killing of Krystle's child, Alexis's engagement to Cecil Colby (Lloyd Bochner) and Cecil's major heart attack, suffered in the throes of lovemaking with Alexis, and so on.

As nefarious and megalomaniacal as the characters were on *Dallas*, the *Dynasty* crew was designed to outdo them. And they did. By mid-December the show was drawing a whopping 35 percent share in the ratings. Suddenly the world was turned upside down for Joan. The woman whom the *National Enquirer* wouldn't bother to interview a few years earlier started to appear on their covers; the woman who used to do her own Christmas shopping and move about unnoticed couldn't go out and mail a letter without attracting a mob, and that bothered her. Joan discovered the downside of stardom. She had always detested crowds, stemming from an incident that occurred at the first premiere she'd attended, when a fan was dragged down the street by the car Joan was in. Now she was practically unable to do anything without making headlines.

But for better or worse, by the end of 1981, at the age of forty-eight and a half, Joan was finally—*finally*—on her way to becoming a superstar. But if stardom was a cure for belt-tightening and exploitation, Joan was about to learn that it came complete with its own set of awful pitfalls.

Chapter Twenty-five

‡‡‡‡‡‡‡‡‡‡‡‡‡‡‡‡‡‡‡‡‡‡‡‡‡‡‡‡‡‡‡‡‡‡‡‡

Joan, Kass, and Katy moved into rented rooms near Fox after Joan started *Dynasty*. Since she'd expected to be going home before too long, no thought had been given to moving there permanently. By December, Joan had to start thinking about it. Alexis had become one of the most popular figures in television.

Joan's Alexis was not great acting. It was scenery eating. As Freddie Francis pointed out, when Joan's on camera, the camera is hers; she's the one audiences watch. And if what Joan was doing in every scene of *Dynasty* wasn't Emmy caliber, it was never uninteresting. A half-smile could usually be found playing about the side of her mouth. Even when she lost her temper, Alexis wasn't fire-angry so much as icily indignant—and menacing. She didn't threaten people: she told them what bad things she was going to do to them, then followed through on her threats. And she did it dressed in clothes that ran the gamut from chic to outrageous; with her pert, erect, confident walk, Joan could wear them all like no one else in television. She'd been on the verge of stardom long enough to know how a poised superstar like Alexis would move.

As the series progressed and Alexis obtained more personal power, she would become less compelling. Someone who has the wealth to crush another person is less fascinating that someone who has only their wits and cool arrogance. But that lay in the future. Toward the end of the season, Joan Collins was on top of the world and once again house-hunting in sunny, mercurial Los Angeles. However, while her career was finally on track, all was far from well in the Kass camp.

The problems of uselessness and alienation Ron had been experiencing in London intensified in Los Angeles, more so now that Joan's every day was so full.

Joan explained, "We work five days a week, with a costume fitting on the sixth day for the week to come. Each day we spend a minimum of twelve hours filming and rehearsing, and I have to get up at five-thirty A.M. When I return home, I feel I must spend all my time with Katy until she goes to bed. After that, I am absolutely shattered. Because I have to look good for my work," she went on, "I need a good eight hours' sleep." The result of this backbreaking schedule didn't leave her with "any time to spend with Ron."

According to Barry Langford, Kass dealt with this and his career problems by comforting himself with cocaine. Pushers would come to the apartment where, says Langford, "Ron took them to quiet corners and money changed hands." Drugs were allegedly everywhere in the house for easy access— even under a mat in the bathroom.

Joan didn't approve, but was too concerned with *Dynasty* to do anything just then. The catalyst occurred one day in the fall when she collapsed on the *Dynasty* set. Langford says, "We all thought she had had a heart attack," and Joan was rushed to the hospital. There, as it turned out, doctors determined that she was suffering from a combination of gastric flu, exhaustion, and tension. Though she was in the process, just then, of suing Newley for back support for the children, what had pushed her over the edge had been an incident in the British press.

Joan had recently signed a contract to publish her third book in May 1982. Called *Katy: A Fight for Life*, it was an expansion of her diaries written in conjunction with her daughter's neurosurgeon, Dr. Robin Illingworth. There had been two reasons for writing the book. The first, she said, was to "pass on . . . advice [and] give hope to other parents who are going through what I went through. Hundreds of children are in this position. If our book helps to save one, it will have been worthwhile." The second reason was so that she could divide whatever monies it earned between charities for disabled children and a trust fund for Katy.

However, her best intentions were to a large degree thwarted when a newspaper reporter interviewed Joan about her career. At the end of their chat, the journalist casually asked how Katy was doing. "It was my reply to this," she realized too late, "and things they already knew about my book and Katy, that the paper used and made them look like the authorized story. The paper even made a television advertisement to plug their story, using a model who looked like me." By so doing, the paper effectively scooped the details of Katy's struggle and destroyed the market for an authorized serialization of Joan's book, which would have generated several thousand dollars for the handicapped. Furious at having been deceived, Joan sued the paper—though the entire affair took a toll on her health.

When she collapsed, says Langford, "The studio rang her home" to inform Kass what had happened. But he "was so far gone on drugs that none of us could wake him to tell him." When Joan was allowed to go home later that day, she arrived to find her husband still asleep. It was then that she realized there was no hope for the marriage, and decided to end it.

In November, with five episodes of *Dynasty* left to shoot, she and Ron separated on a trial basis. "It was a very hard decision to make," she said, but she felt they had to get "some space for a while." However, the trial separation lasted only ten days. Joan had time to be by herself and to think, and what she concluded was that "the thought of a divorce [was] so horrendous" she would rather try to resolve their differences than rend the family apart. "We have a lot of time and experience invested in each other," she said, so "we started going out again. Ron was sweet, and we both made an effort.

"After a few dates," said Joan, "it seemed silly that we should be paying for him to live in an hotel. So he moved back home." Realizing that inactivity was one of his big problems, he also opened an office and, said Joan, was "starting new projects and pulling himself together for the sake of our marriage. He's a marvelous man, not envious or jealous of my success." Unfortunately, Kass would fare no better with this enterprise than he had the last time he tried producing in Los Angeles, and in 1982 their marriage, as well as his state of mind, would go from bad to catastrophic.

Three days after *Dynasty* was finished, Joan flew back to England. She'd committed to do a movie called *Nutcracker* and, while she was there, would be plugging *Dynasty*, which was due to start airing early in 1982.

Back in England, however, all was not well. Not by a long shot.

At the time she left England to make *Dynasty*, one engagement the previous September she could not possibly keep was to appear in Manchester to launch a series of fund-raisers for an organization of the handicapped. James Dowd, secretary of the National Clubland Charity Appeal, said at the time, "We are outraged. Joan was chosen because we thought someone glamourous would ensure the appeal's success. She is letting down thousands of children." The press picked up his complaint, arguing that Joan essentially had sold out the handicapped for the sake of a £500,000 contract.

Hearing of the uproar back in Hollywood, Joan had said, "I'm terribly upset about all this, I have apologized to everybody." She added that her appearance on behalf of the appeals had *always* been contingent on whether or not she was working and, even so, Joan had "begged the producers to let me go." But they had refused. As a *Dynasty* spokesperson had put it, "We're sorry . . . but the show comes first."

It took awhile for the brouhaha to die down, during which time the British newspapers dragged Joan through the mud. But that wasn't all the muckraking they did when she abandoned her homeland yet again. Her finances were also brought before the public. Joan had left behind a trail of investors and creditors who were screaming bloody murder at the actress for having "run out" on them. Heading the list was Phil Green, her partner in the ill-fated Joan Collins Jean Co. Although Joan's signature was stitched onto the seat of a line of jeans, she wasn't around to promote them. That, plus other factors, sent the company under. "I expect I will have lost between three hundred and four hundred thousand pounds," complained Green. "She was keen at the start, but then she landed the part in *Dynasty* and went off to live in California."

People of lesser means were also unhappy with Joan. She left England owing milkman Brian Robinson £23, newsagent Jean Lambkin £20, and gardener Tony Chatsfield nearly £200. Mr. Robinson quipped, "Joan might be a star, but I can tell you she is not that popular round here." While it's possible that Joan, preoccupied with drumming up work in England, was unaware of the bills at first, it would be months before anyone was paid. This was not malice but neglect; Joan was very caught up in the idea of being a star.

Thus, when Joan returned at year's end, she had to face the music. The smaller bills got paid, but about the charity row she became positively indignant. "No one seems interested in the fact that I did twenty-five charity shows in the previous twelve months, and for four years I've supported financially a child in Biafra. I've never made a big deal about it," she growled, "yet there I am being called 'uncaring' and 'a witch' because I had to go off and work." She underscored her indignation about that and other negative reports of her in the British press by snapping, "I seem to have this image of a sort of scarlet woman over here. This is rubbish. I've had enough [and] I'll have to start suing these sons-of-bitches."

She would make good on that promise a year later, but for now she was content to try to ignore them while making the movie, publicizing the show, and talking up the project that was even closer to her heart—*Katy: A Fight for Life*.

Following her hectic and tiring trip to England, Joan bought a big house in Coldwater Canyon, high in the Hollywood Hills and not far from where sister Jackie lived. Though Tara and Sacha were living in Europe—Tara attending an American school in Paris, and Sacha at boarding school in Leicestershire, England—they would be visiting from time to time and Joan wanted elbow room. To make sure that this time, at least, she had the money to keep the place running, she did a pair of innocuous TV movies: *The Paper Dolls*, which aired in May 1982 and was about a pair of young models (Daryl Hannah and Alexandra Paul) who are used by adults and shunned by their friends, and *The Wild Women of Chastity Gulch*, shown in October, about Southern women who must defend their Missouri town against Union soldiers. Though the movies did indeed put a few dollars in her pocket, neither taxed her abilities.

Since there was more time to prepare for the second season of *Dynasty* than there had been for the first, Joan was able to give the writers and designers more input than she had the first time around. She had not been too happy about the costumes during her first shows, which she calls "tacky little suits with fur collars from Saks. I had to make a stand." For the new season, she worked closely with the costumers in designing the wardrobe—budgeted at $15,000 per *episode*—and also made jaunts to Neiman-Marcus to buy clothes off the rack. Scriptwise, Joan said that as she would read through each newly completed teleplay, "change[ing] Alexis's dialogue a lot, hoping to enrich her character, because there's nothing quite so boring as a one-dimensional villain or villainess. I try to bring different shadings to Alexis, particularly humor."

Physically, too, Joan worked hard to get in the best shape of her career. She installed a gym in her home, and worked out almost every day. She also limited her diet to fruit, chicken, and fish, cutting out meat, fat, and sugars. She still drank, but kept that to a minimum.

During this gearing-up period, what was remarkable to Joan was how many "woodwork friends" she suddenly had. When she went out, she expected to see the fans, the "jerks falling over me in restaurants and shops." And while that was often annoying, it didn't bother her nearly as much as the industryites "who a year ago wouldn't cross the street to say hello." She kept at arm's length from those, the ones who had been quick "to gloat over [my] failures," but now wanted to be in her circle.

And there was one thing more Joan did, apart from keeping a small circle of friends, getting into stellar shape, and working hard on the scripts and wardrobe. As Kass would later comment, "*Dynasty* was changing her," but not only in making Joan a more determined professional. "The screen image devoured the *real* woman," he insists. "Joan is superb as the superbitch in *Dynasty*—and she was just as good in the role when we were together at home." He says they actually "had rows in which I found myself telling her, 'Come off it, Alexis.'"

Naturally, Joan denies that she was becoming anything like Alexis. "I can *play* women with balls," she quipped, "but the similarity ends there."

Nonetheless, if the synergy wasn't as strong as Kass paints it, there *were* increasingly striking similarities between the two. Joanisms started to appear in the scripts, cracks about how women can't let men walk over them and about how Alexis's children were the most important things in the world to her—all couched in Joan's own personally witty way. Joan started wearing Alexis's clothes around town, and carrying herself a little bit less like a working actress and more like a star—as on *The Tonight Show* appearance where she actually sat and posed for the audience. Joan denied it over and over, but *all* actors, especially TV actors who play the same part week after week, take as well as they give vis-à-vis their characters. As Charlton Heston once said, "Acting is like picking up a fresh copy of the newspaper: some of the ink is going to come off on your fingers."

Yet, psychologically, perhaps the Joan/Alexis bond was more than that kind of inadvertent give-and-take. On the series, Alexis was frequently referred to as one of the most beautiful women alive. Joan *wanted* to be young and eternally beautiful in real life, and by becoming Alexis she could taste that youth. It was false, of course. As *Rolling Stone* magazine noted in a profile of the actress, "Joan Collins' favorite measurement has to be twelve inches. When you see her from that distance, she really does look beautiful. But from any closer, she looks a bit . . . rough. Her makeup is like a mask: her skin is heavily covered with beige foundation, her eyes are exaggerated by thick shadow, and her lashes stand out like awnings." But Joan wasn't going to be getting closer than twelve inches to anybody. By becoming more like Alexis, she could stay young. And that, for an actress just one year shy of the mid-century mark, was becoming increasingly important.

Chapter Twenty-six

The third season of *Dynasty* had more than its share of melodramatics and surprises.

To begin with, in her second season on the show, Alexis went from being a minor annoyance to a major pain. She had married Cecil Colby in the hospital and actually induced a major heart attack so she'd inherit Colbyco Oil Company—Blake's chief rival. (The ads roared, "She's got Colby's money . . . Colby's power . . . now she wants Blake Carrington's head!") To complicate matters, a young man named Adam (Gordon Thomson) shows up and Fallon falls in love with him—only to learn that he is her brother, the long-lost son of Blake and Alexis. Among the other complications during the season: Alexis learns that Krystle's first marriage may never have been legally annulled and uses the ex-husband for mischief-making, Steven is presumed dead in Indonesia and Blake engages a psychic to help find him, Jeff has a mental breakdown after Adam has his brother-in-law's office redone with poison paint, Blake and Alexis duke-it-out for control of Denver-Carrington, Claudia is put in a sanitarium, Alexis boldly tries to buy that tower-of-power Krystle out of Blake's life, and, as the season ended, Alexis and Krystle were trapped in a burning cabin. Apart from being a means of making sure everyone tuned in the following season, cliffhangers on shows like *Dynasty* and *Dallas* were a means of keeping stars in line. If they asked for too much money, they simply didn't survive the blaze, plane crash, or whatever comparable horror the writers dreamed up.

All of these convolutions— more far-fetched and diabolical than those on other nighttime soap operas—served to make *Dynasty* even more popular, and Joan an even bigger star. In fact, according to John James, who plays Jeff, "Warren Beatty called up one of our producers and told him *Dynasty* was the best regularly scheduled show on television."

Boosting the old home team, perhaps?

With or without Beatty's support, there was no question that Joan would survive the fire. In terms of ratings and the amount of publicity Joan generated, she was worth every penny of the approximately $20,000 an episode they were paying her—which, when it came time to negotiate in April 1983, was more than tripled. As a tribute to how vital she was to the series, that figure was just a few thousand dollars an episode shy of what Larry Hagman was getting for *Dallas*.

But if 1982 was a banner year for Joan professionally, she had more problems than she'd bargained for on the home front. Things weren't going well for Kass. Joan had had a change of heart about publishing *Past Imperfect* in the U.S., and Kass negotiated with Simon and Schuster to have her memoirs published in the fall of 1983. Other than that, however, he managed to stir up little in the way of income. Meanwhile, he was becoming increasingly annoyed with Joan's Alexis-like behavior at home. "Joan refused to admit she had become a bitch toward me," he said. "If we were fighting on the phone she would hang up. If we were face to face, she would get angry and walk away." And when he would tell her that she was behaving like her *Dynasty* alter ego that was, he said, "like using a four-letter word."

Joan, meanwhile, seems to have had her reasons for behaving differently toward her husband. Cocaine aside, according to a report in *The Sun* of London, "Ron . . . delighted in letting men friends see nude pictures of his wife and talking about how good she was in bed." Langford says, "I was disgusted once when he told a male visitor to the house that he was the only man in the U.S. who could satisfy his wildcat wife in the sack." Then, when nude photos of Joan from *The Stud* appeared in a skin magazine—published to capitalize on her newfound supercelebrity status as Alexis—Joan suspected Kass. Though he denies having provided the shots, Joan apparently was not convinced. According to Barry Langford, that "was the beginning of the end. She regarded it as an awful betrayal of trust."

Whether Joan's Alexis-like attitude toward Kass came before or after his "betrayal," not long after *Dynasty* went back into production late in the summer of 1982, she went on what Kass calls a "sex strike. . . . Joan said she didn't feel like making love with me." Kass was upset but says, "I have never been a rapist, so I was going to accept it." There were also reports of impotence, though it isn't clear whether the strike or Kass's striking out came first nor did Joan stop there, according to her husband. In late October of that year, Kass went to London to try to straighten out some of their confused finances and to help arrange a *This Is Your Life* appearance. In order for it to work, the show had to be a surprise, and Kass created a cover of throwing what Joan thought was an eightieth birthday party for her father.

Completing his business, Kass flew back to Los Angeles. When he arrived home, Joan was dressed and asked if he would mind joining her for dinner with her agent and his wife at the trendy Mortons restaurant. Since jet lag had never bothered him, Kass agreed and they all had a delightful time celebrating Joan's success. Then, when it was time to go, Kass remembers, "Joan asked, all matter-of-fact, if I'd like to see an apartment with her. I couldn't understand why, as it was near midnight, but I said, 'Sure.'"

The two drove over to the luxury building on Londonderry View above Sunset, not far from where Joan and Arthur Loew used to rendezvous. When they got there, Joan took out a set of keys and went into one of the apartments.

"This is a very beautiful apartment," Kass told her.

"Yes," she answered, "and I've paid the rent on it for three months for you."

Kass was stunned. He was perversely flattered that she'd taken the time to find a place for him and pay over $1,500 a month for it, but he was sick to be told that "she no longer wanted me under the same roof"—with her or with their daughter—and horrified that "like the ultraorganized Alexis she had planned everything right down to the last detail."

Like the sex strike, however, there was no fighting this. They drove home in silence, where he says he found that he'd already been moved out of their bedroom, a place having been made up in the study until he could pack and get out. The next day, after Joan left for the day's work on *Dynasty*, and Katy was in school, Kass started loading up the station wagon with his belongings. A few days later, Joan changed all the locks in the house, and Kass was not given a key.

There was, at the time, no talk of divorce. Joan still did not want that because of Katy. In fact, when they flew to England a few days later, Joan allegedly pretended for her daughter's sake that all was well between her and Ron. Back at their London home,

Kass says, "We acted out a terrible charade." They would pretend to be living together, and after Katy had gone to bed Kass says he "would duck out to my hotel . . . returning early the next day as though I were staying at the house."

Kass found the separation humiliating and painful. Since there was no keeping the facts from Katy any longer, they took her to a marriage counselor who tried to soften the blow. The arrangement was that Kass would be with Katy on the weekends, and that the three of them would go out to dinner at least once every week. However, said Kass, when he would go to the house Joan would treat him "like something the cat dragged in." He says that she was showing "touches of Alexis more and more," not only in private, when she'd do things like taunting him about other men taking her out, but when she was out in the world—using her name "to get the best table in a restaurant," to avoid waiting in lines for anything, or even to get her car parked.

Returning to his apartment from his visits, Kass says he would feel that "for the first time in my life I was losing control. I was near to committing suicide." The apartment became, in his words, "just like a condemned cell [and] I fell into a deep depression that I've never experienced before. Sometimes I couldn't even bring myself to get out of bed and shave in the morning." (According to Langford, not all of this lassitude was because of depression. He says, "It was nothing unusual for him to be bombed out of his mind, incapable of getting out of bed.)

How much of this was marital strife and how much his alleged use of cocaine is not clear. Regardless, he would eventually begin to rebuild his "shattered life" with a young woman named Mikki Jamison, to whom he was introduced by his lawyer—though not before he had had one final, very public row with his wife.

* * *

Joan went to London twice in the last weeks of 1982, first for the *This Is Your Life* surprise, and then to meet the Queen. During both trips, she managed to get bad and embarrassing press.

The fare for Joan and Katy had been paid for, the first time around, by Rank, producers of *Nutcracker.* For their generosity, Rank had assumed that Joan would be kind enough to mention the film, which was about to open. But she turned against the film when she saw the advertisements that showed her in a leotard and were accompanied by the line, "In *The Stud* she sizzled . . . in *The Bitch* she blazed . . . now in *Nutcracker* Joan Collins breaks all the rules." Rank couldn't understand her displeasure, feeling that the copy was more tasteful that what they'd originally planned ("Her men called her Nutcracker"), but as far as Joan was concerned it was nothing more than "cheap exploitation. It is disgusting and offensive and it makes me mad." So much for goodwill—particularly after a Rank official publicly excoriated her attitude in a newspaper interview.

Worse, however, was the December night when she flew back to host a charity concert by the Royal Philharmonic at London's Albert Hall. Both Queen Elizabeth and Prince Philip were in attendance, and Joan was thrilled and honored to have been selected for the event.

She went to the event with Katy, but no sooner had she stepped out of her Bentley for rehearsals than a High Court writ was pressed into her hand by a private detective. Though Joan didn't know what it was, she shouted, "Don't give it to me! I don't want it!" and threw the documents to the ground. A theater official picked them up. The papers were from Henlys of London, claiming that Joan had never returned an automobile which the manufacturers, British Leyland, had asked them to lend her in exchange for having promoted the new model. But

the loan was to have been for no more than six
months, a period that had expired a year before. Tony
Ball, owner of the firm, said that not only was the car
overdue but his firm had "received thirteen unpaid
parking fines because the car is registered in my
company's name." He added that it hadn't been his
intention to embarrass Joan, but, "We are trying to
run a professional business." He'd had the writ
served because he could still get some £2,000 for the
Mini Metro if it were returned.

However, Joan wasn't only concerned about her
own embarrassment. She thought the car *had* been
returned, and was only too happy to let the owners
have it back. Rather, she was mortified by the
embarrassment the incident would cause the Queen
when the press got hold of it. Rather than go to the
press with a long-winded explanation which would
probably have gotten twisted around, Joan informed
reporters, "I have nothing to say about this. I don't
want to talk to you," and made the necessary
apologies in private.

Meeting the Queen was an extraordinary experience for Joan and especially for her daughter. When
the show was over and they were introduced, royalist
Katy was so overcome by the moment that she
started to cry and had to be comforted by her mother.

More important even than that, however, was that
in spite of the writ and the many low-class films she'd
made over the past decade—first the horror pictures
and then the soft-core porn films—Joan was still
considered classy enough to host the Queen of
England. The strong, elegant image of Alexis had
enabled her to transcend not merely the reality of her
age but any and all misdeeds as well. And she was
still only shooting her second season with the show!

But there was a trap as well, the danger that the
image was so strong Joan would be typecast for life.
For that reason, as soon as there was a break in the
Dynasty shoot, she undertook one of the most remarkable roles of her career.

Chapter Twenty-seven

◆◆◆◆◆◆◆◆◆◆◆◆◆◆◆◆◆◆◆◆◆◆◆◆◆◆◆◆◆◆◆◆◆◆◆◆◆◆◆

When actress Shelley Duvall launched her *Faerie Tale Theatre* series for airing over cable on Showtime and release on videocassette, she signed a minimum of one major star for each release: Christopher Reeve for *Sleeping Beauty*, Malcolm McDowell and wife Mary Steenburgen for *Little Red Riding Hood*, Elliot Gould and Jean Stapleton in *Jack and the Beanstalk*, Tatum O'Neal for *Goldilocks and the Three Bears*. For *Hansel and Gretel*, Duvall also approached two top stars: Joan Collins and Joan Collins.

Joan was cast as both the wicked stepmother who sent the children into the forest to die when food got scarce and the witch who tried to cook them for her own meals.

Scowling and talking in clipped, sneering tones, Joan was nasty enough as the stepmother, but as the witch she was positively brilliant. She wore a great deal of makeup to look like a traditional witch: hooked nose, knobby chin, wrinkles, spindly fingers, and long, stringy hair beneath a pointed hat. Walking stooped over, Joan alternately narrowed and widened her eyes as she made Gretel work for her and cackled in a wonderfully broken voice about the badness of children and the pleasures of turning them into gingerbread. Joan was particularly effective in the scene where she beamed to Gretel about the positive joy of having "mountains of young boy flesh" to eat. Any similarity between the witch and the actress was, of course, purely in the mind of the viewer.

Though *Hansel and Gretel* was shot in under a week, and Joan was burdened under a hot, uncomfortable latex nose and chin and layers of costuming, she had not enjoyed a part so much in years. Her delight shows; if ever anyone doubted that Joan could slip into a character role and totally obliterate the glamour-girl image, this performance was evidence of her talent.

For Joan, 1983 opened with a bang—the kind to which she was becoming increasingly accustomed—and continued at a litigious, angry pace on several different fronts.

The biggest problem was one that literally left her reeling because of its scope and because it took her utterly by surprise. As London's *Sunday People* put it in a spectacular headline, "DYNASTY'S JOAN SUED FOR £228,000."

At issue was nearly a half-million dollars being sought in an action started by City of London bankers Hill Samuel and Company. The firm claimed that the Kasses owed them that much money for three years and that interest was accruing at the staggering rate of £87 a *day*. Upon hearing about it, Joan flew to England to confer with her attorney, Roger Lane-Smith. Implying that this was one of Kass's dealings, not hers, Joan insisted through Lane-Smith that she was "not involved" in this latest episode of financial impropriety, and the claim was contested. According to Kass, however, the beef was legitimate, and whether Joan liked it or not the money would somehow have to be repaid.

Ron said that when they had returned to London to live in 1979, "We borrowed for two homes in Britain." The actual figures, at the time, were £50,000 and £25,000. "When our daughter Katy was desperately ill," he went on, "both Joan and I gave up our careers to be with her and we got behind with the repayments." As he girded his loins to deal with the problem, Kass wisecracked to a trio of reporters that while personal problems had torn them apart, financial problems were forcing them to stay in touch.

Whether or not Joan was ignorant of those outstanding loans, Kass had yet another surprise in store for her—this one more personally devastating.

When they separated, Joan and Kass had agreed that in the best interests of their daughter, they would, in Joan's words, "draw up a document, which we both signed, in which we agreed that neither of us would *ever* say anything derogatory about the other which could influence Katy's feelings about her mother or father."

In spite of this, in April Kass submitted to a series of interviews with members of the British press in which he went into detail about his life with Joan, and about some of the problems they had. Included in his *Sunday People* pieces were mild revelations about their sex life, comments such as, "Her sex drive was not as strong as mine . . . but what was lacking in quantity was made up for in quality," and spoke longingly of her nighttime attire, like "expensive sensual nighties." He stated unequivocally that no other woman could look "as devastating as Joan in a chic black *see*-through nightgown slit to the thigh." He added that if she came to bed wearing that, he knew "we were going to have a great night."

The first article appeared on May 1, and when Joan heard about it she hit the roof. Not only did he unbare their private life but he speculated at length on how much like the bitchy Alexis she was becoming—material she definitely did *not* want Katy to read or, one assumes, the public either. "I am deeply hurt," she said, viewing it as a breach of faith and because "it was so important to Katy that Ron and I should remain friends." That, apparently, was now no longer possible in her view, though one of the contentions of Kass's articles was that he and Joan hadn't been friends for a while.

More than that, however, Joan was worried that Katy might be "deeply and traumatically upset" to read such things about her mother, and went to London to try, legally, to bar future articles. A half-day was set aside for a private hearing on *Kass vs. Kass* in a London court, but it never got that far. Meeting for an hour before they went in to see the judge about an injunction, Joan's attorneys and those from the newspaper managed to reach a less severe resolution. The deal they struck, according to a joint statement, was that publication could continue "on the basis of certain assurances being given by the defendants as to the contents of future installments in the series." In other words, parts strenuously objected to by Joan would be excised.

With that out of the way, Joan was so annoyed by Kass in general that she applied her energies to pursuing what, in spite of everything, she had never really wanted—her third divorce. Kass was not surprised, having steeled himself for this and his other pressures by seeking a psychiatrist's care and enrolling at the Shrublands health farm in East Anglia. Still, what Joan had hoped would be an amicable split got messy when, early in 1984, Kass went to court to try to get spousal support. Although admitting he wasn't broke— "I've a first class art collection and Beatles memorabilia which in itself must be worth a small fortune"—he was cash-poor and still nearly $40,000 in debt. Crying poverty as "a procedural matter," he tried to get Joan to ante up nearly $8,000 a month. Although Joan wasn't pleased to be asked to support yet another husband, she willingly lent him nearly $20,000 interest-free to help him out of his hole. Although they were officially divorced in May, Kass continued to press his case over the division of property and income.

Unfettered and still in a fighting mood, Joan turned her spleen on a columnist for the *Daily Mirror*, Anne

Robinson, who had suggested in her column that Joan was being unfair to Kass. Joan's letter, which the paper published, was unusually harsh. However, she had had her fill of over a quarter-century of hounding from the British press.

"This is just another example of the atrociously lazy journalistic habits of so-called responsible newspaper people," she wrote in part. "I would like a retraction of your disgusting allegations . . . and for your further information, I do not use 'half-a-dozen layers of tarantula-like eyelashes'—nor do I use three or four switches of hair." She concluded by stating, "The amusing thing about your incompetent Fleet Street vermin is that you are far, far bitchier about me and others in my profession than we could ever be."

To which the battle-seasoned Ms. Robinson replied snidely, "Dear Joan: If I had some false eyelashes I'd weep into them."

Though that bout has to be classified as a draw, Joan was satisfied enough to go out and, next, launch what she felt was a long-overdue attack on the entire British press and their attitude toward her. For years, thanks to her movie of the same name, "Bitch" and "Joan Collins" had been synonymous in the British press. Even during the uproar over Kass's articles, the papers reported them with headlines like, "THE BITCH GAGS HER KISS-TELL HUSBAND" and "THE BITCH BITES BACK." She wanted it stopped. As she told one sympathetic reporter, "I wasn't so much upset for myself as for my children. They were being taunted at school. It can be very hurtful for a child to have other youngsters chanting, 'Your mother's a bitch.'" Thus, Lane-Smith dispatched a letter to all the offending papers, an icy document which read, in part:

The fact that in 1978 our client played a nightclub proprietor in the film called *The Bitch* does not, in our view, entitle journalists to continually refer to her in this derogatory manner. We write to you in the hope that you will accept our client's wish that the practice of reference to her as the Bitch ceases.

Rather than buckle to the implied threat of legal action, one paper, the *Star*, put it to a vote among its readers. And when the tally came in favoring Joan's request, the paper conceded defeat by wickedly running the following headline: "OK, JOAN, YOU WIN. WE WON'T CALL YOU THE BITCH ANY MORE." Instead, when they ran a picture of Joan with one of her male friends, they captioned it, "JOAN'S NEW STUD."

Even then, Joan was not through throwing her weight around. In the midst of all this turmoil with Kass and with the press, Joan also went into the ring with the *Dynasty* producers over the matter of her salary for the 1983–84 season. In February she had dumped longtime agent Korman to sign with the powerful William Morris Agency and, well aware of her value to the show, Joan reportedly asked Aaron Spelling for nearly $100,000 an episode. According to a report in London's *Daily Mirror*, producer Spelling was far from pleased and responded by telling his scriptwriters to "write her role out." Since Alexis had been left in a burning cabin and *could* be easily replaced by another bitch, Joan quickly clarified her position by stating that, yes, there was a "renegotiation" in process but, no, she had "no plans to leave the show. I've never walked out on a contract in my life."

While Triumph in London and the sponsors of her aborted Chicago stage play might dispute that claim, Joan was sincere about wanting to stay. Kass had said in one of his articles that "she has become obsessed with money," and she wasn't about to kill her golden goose. According to *Rolling Stone*, she ended up with some $45,000 a show.

Joan may well have been just a few weeks away

from the half-century mark when she began her slew
of crusades, but never had she been more of a
dynamo, shooting from one to the other to the next,
hardly pausing for breath between them. "I have a
superabundance of energy," she boasted, promulgat-
ing the impression of youthful vim. "I know I can
make things work out."

And so she did, but not in the pouty, long-suffering
manner of the woman who had had to sit idle on the
Fox lot for a year or make *Empire of the Ants*. In peace
she was still the clever, charming individual she'd
always been. But in war, she was pure Alexis.

Chapter Twenty-eight

*A*s a tribute to Joan's for-
titude, not only was she able to thrust and parry on a
variety of fronts but she was able to keep working
and loving the entire time.

In addition to finishing up her second season of
Dynasty, Joan made a TV movie that created more
steam offscreen than it did on. The picture, originally
entitled *Beefcake*, then *The Look*, finally aired in October as *The Making of a Male Model*. The ABC presenta-
tion starred Jon-Erik Hexum (of the season's ill-fated
series *Voyagers*) as a dashing stunt pilot who becomes
a model, with Joan featured (for $100,000) as his
mentor-cum-lover Kay Dillon.

As soon as the tall, jut-jawed Hexum and the
newly liberated Joan met, they became an item. The
fact that he was approximately half her age didn't
bother either of them. Like Warren Beatty before him,

Hexum got press coverage being seen with Joan; for her part, he enhanced Joan's reputation as a woman who was getting younger all the time. Which is not to imply that they didn't care for each other. But going out obviously afforded benefits which went beyond pure romance, a fact underscored by the way the relationship cooled as quickly as it had begun—coincidentally, not long after Hexum lost a part on *Dynasty*.

During the summer, the producers of *Dynasty* were casting about for a hunk to play a new character named Dexter, Alexis's young partner and lover. There were two actors in the running: rugged Michael Nader, of *Bare Essence*, and Hexum. According to sources on the show, Joan pushed for Hexum to be cast. And she could indeed push. She had a lot of clout with the producers and those stores of Alexis-like strength. So intimidating could she be, in fact, that in London the *Guardian* wrote of a public relations man who had disappointed her and was so terrified that he "tried to sink into the cushions of the settee like a Wurlitzer organ disappearing into a cinema stage." But the *Dynasty* producers bit the bullet and turned her down on Hexum. Not that they weren't high on him. They were simply afraid that if anything went wrong with the Collins/Hexum romance, it would be impossible for them to work together on the set. The part went to Nader and, prophetically, Hexum and Joan parted company not long after.

Joan didn't seem terribly distraught by the break-up. Within weeks she had herself a brand-new boyfriend, a singer who was equally as young (thirty-six), equally as lantern-jawed, and equally as visible in the press thanks to his association with Joan. He was also the source of some very unwelcome and sensational headlines at year's end.

His name was Peter Holm, and Joan met him in London quite by accident. "I'd taken a house in the country to spend some time with the children," she says, "and . . . burglars got in. After that I didn't fancy staying in the house so I went back to London and spent a day at a friend's house. That was where I met Peter, by the swimming pool."

Joan says that her first impression of the blue-eyed Holm was mixed. "Lying by the pool was this tall blond hunk, who looked sort of cute, but I decided he had absolutely no personality because he did not speak all day." Then, she said, he began playing the guitar "and he was brilliant." Though she had no intention of jumping back into a relationship, she asked him to escort her to a movie opening and, after that, as it so often did with the men in her life, things just happened. They found themselves chatting after the film, and when Joan returned to Los Angeles she found herself thinking about Holm a great deal. For his part, the Swede hadn't been looking for anything beyond a pleasant evening and the prospect of possibly going to bed with her ("I thought if she's like the character in *The Stud* it could happen," he admits). But when they had their little talk, he found himself as entranced by Joan's mind as he was with her body.

Holm insists that, like Joan, he hadn't intended to fall in love. That simply wasn't his style. "I have been a bit of a bastard to women in the past," he acknowledges, "and I have had hundreds of girl-friends." Joan, however, was different from the others.

They didn't end up in bed that night but, visiting Joan in Los Angeles, Holm ended up staying with her for nearly a month. And during that time they got hooked. She was happy because, apart from liking the same foods, music, and people as she, he didn't try to dominate her the way other men had. In fact, he inadvertently helped her along the path to Alexis-dom by encouraging Joan, in her words, to be less "scatterbrained about my finances and my business and to take control of my affairs." For Holm's part, he found Joan "the most many-sided woman I've ever met . . . the most soft and hard, most loving and tough woman," and stated, "This is the first time in my life I am really in love." Holm was also a big hit with Katy, not only because he was personable and handsome, but because, in his opinion, the eleven-year-old was happy to see her mother so content with him.

While she was suddenly serious about Holm, she *said* that she very definitely drew the line at marriage. "One should always be in love," she said. "That is why one should never marry." She didn't want to ruin the relationship by formalizing it, and then face the prospect of going through yet another divorce. Besides, she had come to the conclusion that being married didn't leave enough time for herself. "We all have a certain built-in selfishness," she said. "Even if we say we love someone totally we really put ourselves first." Away from Kass, she'd found a great deal of pleasure in "the total freedom of going anywhere and doing anything without reference to anyone else," and wasn't willing to give that up.

In September he moved in with her and, despite her protestations, there *was* some talk of marriage. However, things briefly soured in their Coldwater Canyon Shangri-La that November when Holm was summoned to Stockholm. It turned out that back in 1975 he had been accused of smuggling $2 millions' worth of diamonds from Belgium into Sweden, and had allegedly jumped bail and left the country. Though Joan flew over with him, they stood some thirty feet apart when changing planes at Heathrow in London so that photographers could not shoot them together. Whether Joan did that to spite her old nemeses, or simply didn't want to be photographed with a potential criminal isn't certain, nor did it prevent such headlines in England as "JOAN'S NEW LOVE IS ON THE RUN" and "JOAN FLIES IN WITH A

FUGITIVE." But the matter of Holm's past was quietly and secretly cleared up and the couple were soon back in Los Angeles, where they were once more standing close enough together to be photographed, and he was suddenly serving as her most trusted business adviser.

While 1983 proved a tumultuous year in many respects, one area where Joan had no complaints was in the licensing department. In July, a month before Joan began working on her third season of *Dynasty*, she started to enjoy some of the *real* perks of her newfound fame: endorsing products for big bucks.

To begin with, Revlon hired her to promote their glamourous new perfume Scoundrel, for which she was reportedly paid $1 million a year for a two-year deal. She was also given a hefty sum to plug Cannon Mills products in ads which suggestively announced, "Two of the most famous names in America bathe together." Next, she introduced the Joan Collins Collection of costume jewelry through Designer Lines, Inc. And finally, the Cinzano campaign was resurrected, and early in 1984 Joan filmed new commercials—reportedly at a much higher fee. Like *Hansel and Gretel*, these continued to show that for all her offscreen Alexis-isms, Joan was able to poke fun at herself: In the first of the new spots, not only did Leonard Rossiter trip on a rug and douse the elegant Joan with Cinzano, but a group of Japanese onlookers, mistaking his action for a ritual of some kind, followed suit. Joan's stiff-upper-lip poise during these calamities proved that her greatest talents do indeed lie in comedy, and it's unfortunate that being typecast as a "sex bomb" has allowed her to do so little of it. Indeed, as Joan began gearing up for *Dynasty*, about the only thing which continued to elude her was the chance to do quality work.

Joan plunged with enthusiasm into a new series of *Dynasty* adventures. The actress once described Alexis as being "pure as the driven slush," and in the show's fourth season Ms. Colby certainly lived up to the description. Indeed, after watching Alexis at work this season, Bendix Corporation ex-vice-president Mary Cunningham was moved to write in *TV Guide*, "Alexis . . . embodies all that is wrong with female executives on television today. She is not above using sex and blackmail to close important deals." Nor did she hesitate to order her employees to use sex to get vital information from the Carrington clan. Joan even got to sing in a saloon scene—something she hadn't done since her film with Newley.

Having survived the inferno set at the end of the previous season, Alexis hires (and seduces) a body-guard named Mark (Geoffrey Scott) after she is stalked by a killer in the hospital and the victim of a robbery attempt. She then gets blackmailed herself into taking the blame for trying to poison Jeff, falls in love with newcomer Dex, who is the son of a Denver-Carrington board member (the ads that week screamed, "The heat is on! Alexis lights her new man's *fire!*"), gets to meet Gerald R. Ford and Henry Kissinger at Denver's Carousel Ball, and is nearly shot to death by the daughter of a man whose death she helped to cause. To Joan's credit, she allowed Alexis to be very human when faced with the pistol, giving the viewer the rare opportunity of seeing her flustered and frightened for a few moments—before she sweet-talks the girl into handing her the weapon.

At the end of the season, the producers left Alexis in a singularly tight spot. However, this time they had more than just the potential for contract problems to worry about. They were also concerned about the series' survival. Though *Dynasty* remained at the top of the ratings pile, Joan was everywhere in 1983–84—so overexposed that *People* magazine readers voted her the most overrated female star extant. So well known was she that comedians started using her in their routines; for example, at a Friars Club Roast of the L.A. Raiders, Milton Berle quipped, "This is the first time the Friars have had an affair with an entire football team . . . which is more than Joan Collins can say." She was on the best-seller lists with her autobiography, did every talk show as she promoted the book, appeared nude in a *Playboy* spread in December 1983, co-starred in yet another made-for-TV movie, (*My Life as a Man*, made in March 1984), did another special (*Blondes vs. Brunettes*, in May, in which she acted the role of Krystle in a *Dynasty* spoof, Morgan Fairchild playing Alexis), got a star on the Walk of Fame in Hollywood, and was seen in print and on TV endorsing Cannon, British Airways, and Scoundrel. She was even roasted by Dean Martin, Milton Berle, Angie Dickinson, Phillis Diller, and others in a prime-time special, enduring lines like "Joan has been in more hotel rooms than the Gideon Bible," "Joan only smokes cigarettes after making love, so she's down to two packs a day," and "Towels in her home are marked, 'Hers' and 'Next.'" She reportedly wasn't too pleased with the vulgar tone of the show, but she said she had to "accept that people see me as notorious. . . . It's not the way I see myself, but I can see how people see that because I'm not a retiring violet." For a fee in the neighborhood of $75,000, she grinned and bore it.

Joan also managed to get in the news for virtually everything she did, whether it was giving *Dynasty* crew members a Christmas gift which they felt was unutterably cheap (a T-shirt that said "Merry Christmas from Joan Collins"), storming out of a Beverly Hills boutique in April because she'd forgotten her check-cashing card and the clerk wouldn't take her check ("What! Don't you know who I am?" she screamed at the unimpressed man behind the counter), and going discoing on two consecutive nights with Mercedes-Benz heir Muck Flick (firing empty speculation about the status of the Holm relationship). She received especially widespread coverage over potshots she took at *Dallas* star Larry Hagman and her fellow Britons.

Of Hagman, she said they'd been at a party and was shocked to find him "talking and acting like the character he plays. He was just so overbearing and so stupid, using a phony accent which I know he doesn't have." With total disregard of her own hunchback, she said, "The man has totally believed his own publicity."

She had even harsher words for the English. "They don't want to work," she said. "All people in Britain want to do these days is lie around and watch TV. [They're] so fucking soft it makes me puke." (Her broadside drew the following irate reply from Member of Parliament Geoffrey Dickens: "These British people that make her puke are also paying her wages. I don't know when Joan Collins was last in a factory here, but I can assure her that the British workman is anything but soft.")

Whether she was speaking well or ill of people, Joan was being quoted—ironic, considering that for the first few months that she was shooting *Dynasty*, ABC couldn't get her any press coverage. Now, even Joan's ex-cook and ex-valet Mena and John Bevan got press coverage when they talked about her habits, such as how Joan enjoyed entertaining people at her home by showing them episodes of *Dynasty* in advance of their airing and, according to John, so doing in a "shiny, snake-tight creation which accentuates her hills and valleys." And not only was she in the legitimate press, but managed to make one or the other of the scandal sheets at least once a week.

Quite understandably, the *Dynasty* producers must have been afraid that she was going to wear out her welcome with the public. And if that happened, the show could well sink to its pre-Alexis levels. Then, too, there *were* money problems. Though she had a year to go on her contract, in February Joan herself apparently started rumors that she was going to be starring in ten episodes of a new show called *Vixen* at $120,000 per episode. Though Joan was already pulling down nearly $50,000 per episode on *Dynasty*, columnist Liz Smith wrote that "making the *Dynasty* people nervous is one of her pastimes," and talk of defecting to *Vixen* for a lot of money was calculated to do just that.

In light of all this, the producers decided that it was time for a new rich bitch to appear in Denver: Dominique Deveraux (Diahann Carroll), with added star-power provided by Billy Dee Williams as her husband. Concurrently, they ended the season with Alexis in a desperate situation. After underhandedly leaving Blake on the verge of bankruptcy by meddling in a foreign oil deal, she is blackmailed by Mark, who has overheard her plotting. Shortly thereafter, Mark is killed in a fall from Alexis's balcony and his employer is charged with the crime. When the season ended, Alexis found herself locked up with hookers and other less-than-elegant types, screaming out her innocence.

Not surprisingly, though Joan was still appearing everywhere, talk of *Vixen* slowly petered out.

Epilogue

＊＊＊

*A*lexis was back when the series returned in the fall of 1984 and the *Dynasty* development actually appealed to Joan. She had long wanted to expand Alexis beyond being just a black widow, and having her imprisoned and down for the count was a good way to do it. The murder and the presence of the even cooler Dominique showcased Alexis's more desperate side, allowing Joan to do some acting. With all her satisfaction at the wealth and fame Alexis had brought her, Joan knew that the character was suffocating her. She had to stretch it or die.

Still, there is some question as to whether Joan will want to survive yet *another* cliffhanger at the end of the next season. "I'm just a *Dynasty*—slave," she quips, and has said she wants to do no more than a few years of *Dynasty* and then "get out before the public becomes sick of me." Her ambition, she says, is "to do one terrific film, something I could show my grandchildren and say, 'This is what Granny did.' I want to do something special [and] I think maybe in 1985 I will."

That all but excludes TV, she continues, because it "eats you up and spits you out." While she still makes the occasional TV movie like *The Cartier Affair* with *Knight Rider*'s David Hasselhoff, the essence of the medium, she has discovered, is to make someone "the flavor of the month or maybe the flavor of the year, but next year or the year after another flavor will come along." After four years of *Dynasty*, she has had quite enough of that. "Something special" also virtually excludes the theater, for while it is still her "first love" she is reluctant to go back because "I can't make the kind of living there I'm used to making." Broadway is the exception, and she has hopes of someday appearing there.

In the meantime, Joan believes that the only way she'll have any chance of achieving her goals will be, in her words, to "continue to look attractive enough to play forty-year-olds when I'm sixty." To this end, she took the rather radical step of posing both nude and semiclad for *Playboy*. Joan said the spread was an effort to strike a blow for women who tend to feel washed up once they leave their forties behind. She told columnist Unity Hall, "It's a significant step for feminism," the journalist further describing the move as "a positive two-finger gesture to all those who believe women really ought to grow older gracefully, and preferably out of sight."

However, as much as Joan did it to fight the demon of "ageism" which hinders others, she also did it to show how young *she* looked. The issue was a sellout and Joan's image as a forty-year-old was given a huge boost. This was abetted by flattering comments that appeared in the press courtesy of *Playboy* photographer Mario Cassilli, remarks such as, "There is a little bit of animal in her that she lets sneak out," and, "You feel as if you are with a panther." Joan was on the prowl—not only for men but for youth.

Michael Winner recalls a little bash he threw a few years ago. "Joan was very hot on *Dynasty*, and I gave a little party on a boat in the Thames. She came, with the wind blowing and her hair all a mess, but she was immensely jolly, singing Cockney songs with the people on the boat. There was no attempt to preserve glamour or worry about her hair being out of place." It was a sorority kind of attitude she had, a college girl on a lark; not Alexis but the kind of free-spirited character she'd played in *I Believe in You* and *The Square Ring*.

"For an actress," she told Johnny Carson that night she went on like a queen, "I think I'm pretty well balanced. I think the main thing is to realize that you may be here today and could quite easily be gone tomorrow, but you may be back the day after."

She's right. And for all her eccentricities, Joan is more resilient than almost any other star of her era.

At the end of *Land of the Pharaohs*, Nellifer is imprisoned in the pyramid of her dead husband. As the stones are lowered, she runs around screaming at the top of her lungs, "I don't want to die! I don't want to die!" Apparently, Joan has learned her lesson from the doomed queen. With the walls of age and typecasting closing in on her, Joan is constantly on the run. She works at staying beautiful and she thinks young. She helps her mind and emotions stay vital by changing jobs and lovers and residences with regularity. Whether it's Gemini-inspired fickleness, as she claims, or temperament, as some of her directors claim, or simply a remarkable instinct for survival, Joan never stops.

And, more important, nothing stops her.

ABOUT THE AUTHOR

Jeff Rovin is the author of over thirty books. Among them are historical novels, science fiction, and books on film and TV, including ALWAYS, LANA (with Taylor Pero), and THE FILMS OF CHARLTON HESTON, written with the actor's cooperation. Rovin has also written about celebrities for *The Ladies' Home Journal, Omni, Moviegoers,* and *USA Today*, and published the topselling monthly magazine *Videogaming Illustrated*.

OUT ON A LIMB
by Shirley MacLaine

Her courageous and controversial bestseller.

In this remarkable and moving story we are invited to accompany world-famous actress Shirley MacLaine on a unique journey – to Stockholm, where she meets a trance channeler whose unusual gift opens the door to her past; to Europe and Hawaii, where a secret (and perhaps fated) affair of the heart unfolds; and finally to Peru, where high in the mountains she has a startling out-of-body experience that clarifies for her the extent of human potential and the understanding that the soul lives forever.

Out On A Limb is the deeply personal story of a woman determined to know herself and to become all she is capable of being. Shirley MacLaine, author of two previous bestsellers, *Don't Fall Off The Mountain* and *You Can Get There From Here*, has opened her heart more than ever before, and her story is unforgettable.

'Highly entertaining'
The Guardian

0 552 12452 4   £2.50

AND I DON'T WANT LIVE THIS LIFE
Deborah Spungen

'Harrowing, brutally honest and beautifully written'
Woman

They called her 'Nauseating Nancy' – the outrageous girlfriend of Sex Pistol Sid Vicious. She died as she had lived – shockingly, in a sleazy New York hotel. Sid would be charged with her murder before his own untimely death. But what the lurid headlines didn't reveal was the family heartbreak behind the horror: 19 years of struggling to understand a daughter who, even as a toddler, rebelled against everything her parents stood for. Now, at last, her mother has broken the silence . . .

And I Don't Want To Live This Life is a powerful and moving insight into the structure of a modern family. It is a twentieth century tragedy, whose final message shining through the darkness is one of hope.

'One of the most heart-rending books a mother has ever written about a daughter'
Daily Mirror

'A most remarkable book . . . a harrowingly honest, hypnotically readable account of a modern tragedy'
Dublin Evening Herald

'Engrossing where you expect it to be superficial, harrowing where you expect it to be harmless and a testament of the will which battled against the obvious conclusion to Nancy's life, which was fraught with unpredictable violence and could only be expected to end within those confines'
Time Out

0 552 12589 X   £2.50

CATCH A FIRE
The Life of Bob Marley
by Timothy White

'Superb . . . as fine and moving a biography as Marley could have wanted'
New Musical Express

Bob Marley – undisputed sovereign of reggae music, the pre-eminent political visionary of the Third World, a revolutionary soul-prophet whose music had a massive impact on people of all races throughout the world. His death from cancer at the age of thirty-six in 1981 was mourned by the millions who were inspired by his vision and mesmerised by his haunting power.

Catch A Fire – a vivid and dramatic chronicle of Bob Marley's life and career, from poverty in Kingston's Trench Town to international superstardom. An insightful exploration of the historical, cultural, religious and folkloric milieu that shaped Marley's spiritual and political beliefs and out of which the uniquely Jamaican version of rock music, later known as reggae, was spawned.

*MANY NEVER-BEFORE-SEEN PHOTOGRAPHS
*THE FIRST COMPLETE DISCOGRAPHY
*EXHAUSTIVE BIBLIOGRAPHY

'Exhaustively researched . . . brilliant . . . spellbinding and authoritative'
Time Out

'So vivid and authoritative is White's work that it's certain to beome the yardstick by which others are judged'
Black Music

0 552 99097 3   £3.95

A SELECTED LIST OF
AUTOBIOGRAPHIES AND BIOGRAPHIES
AVAILABLE FROM CORGI/BANTAM

WHILE EVERY EFFORT IS MADE TO KEEP PRICES LOW, IT IS SOME-
TIMES NECESSARY TO INCREASE PRICES AT SHORT NOTICE. CORGI
BOOKS RESERVE THE RIGHT TO SHOW NEW RETAIL PRICES ON
COVERS WHICH MAY DIFFER FROM THOSE PREVIOUSLY ADVERTISED
IN THE TEXT OR ELSEWHERE.

THE PRICES SHOWN BELOW WERE CORRECT AT THE TIME OF GOING
TO PRESS (JANAUARY '85).

*All these books are available at your book shop or newsagent, or can be ordered
direct from the publisher. Just tick the titles you want and fill in the form below.*

CORGI BOOKS, Cash Sales Department, P.O. Box 11, Falmouth, Cornwall.

Please send cheque or postal order, no currency.

Please allow cost of book(s) plus the following for postage and packing:

U.K. Customers—Allow 55p for the first book, 22p for the second book and 14p for
each additional book ordered, to a maximum charge of £1.75.

B.F.P.O. and Eire—Allow 55p for the first book, 22p for the second book plus 14p
per copy for the next seven books, thereafter 8p per book.

Overseas Customers—Allow £1.00 for the first book and 25p per copy for each
additional book.

NAME (Block Letters) ....

ADDRESS ....

....